STEHEKIN
A Valley in Time

STEHEKIN
A Valley in Time

Grant McConnell

The Mountaineers/Seattle

The Mountaineers: Organized 1906 ". . . to explore, study, preserve, and enjoy the natural beauty of the Northwest."

2   1   0   9   8
5   4   3   2   1

Published by The Mountaineers
306 Second Avenue West, Seattle, Washington 98119

Published simultaneously in Canada by Douglas & McIntyre, Ltd.,
1615 Venables Street, Vancouver, B.C. V5L 2H1

Manufactured in the United States of America

Edited by Lynelle Diamond
Cover art by Sukey Forsman
Endpaper map by Newell Cartographics

Chapter 7 first appeared in *The Virginia Quarterly Review,* 1962.

Library of Congress Cataloging-in-Publication Data

McConnell, Grant.
    Stehekin, a valley in time / Grant McConnell.
       p.   cm.
    ISBN 0-89886-181-0 :
    1. Stehekin (Wash.)--Social life and customs.   2. Mountain life-
-Washington (State)--Stehekin.   3. McConnell, Grant   I. Title.
    F899.S84M37 1988
    979.7'59--dc19   88-9095
                                                              CIP

For Jane especially

1.

There was a time
and there wasn't a time—

so runs the folk tale beginning. It's proper here,
for there was a time, the end of World War II,
and there wasn't a time, just the American past.
But there was a place—one unique and beautiful, as perhaps most places of the earth once
were, but known to only a few.

No road reached it from outside. This was
enough in the middle of the twentieth century to
render it remote and little touched by the cur-
rents of American life racing past the mountain
barriers around it. And this was ironic, for its
name, Stehekin, means "the way through." It is

an Indian name, and maybe it tells the whole of an epoch—
that the bands that came were mere travelers, outriders of a
nomadic people whose true life lay on the rolling plains to
the east, where the sun beats down without shadow from
dawn until dusk. Perhaps they came to trade with the people
of the dark and humid western slope, where human suste-
nance was based on the sea and the waters that feed into it.
Or maybe they simply came adventuring and hurried out
again with big stories of what they had done. There are faint
remains of pictures on some of the rocks near Stehekin;
"paintings," they are usually called, but maybe they were just
grafitti; the one that could be read until not long ago seemed
to be a brag about somebody's hunt.

Their route was fairly obvious, the first part of it at least. It
began on the shelf of land hanging onto the uplift of the Cascade Range west of the Columbia, really a part of the inland
plateau but sliced off from the rest by the river. There is a
lake here that drains down through a series of falls into the
Columbia six hundred feet below. It's a pleasant sight, particularly when seen after hours—or days—of travel through
the plains. In summer it has a nice jade cast but there is nothing about it to justify the translation of "bubbling water"
given to its name, Chelan; that's just translator poetry. The
lake closes off in the middle distance; pine-covered hills rise
beyond.

It's not hard to imagine the Indians out on the lake in their
canoes. These would have been pretty solid and well designed, made for shooting the Columbia down below after
having been hauled up from the river and over the lip of an
old moraine that blocks the foot of the lake. Perhaps the Indians would be out fishing and would reach what looked like

the far end. And then, what looked like the end would turn out to have an opening, and they would see the lake going on around a bend and then a long stretch of water like the one they had just paddled up, only with bigger hills than those they had seen from below. So they might camp on a little point of land, a good place with level ground and a few tall trees for shade and wood. And next day when they would go on the new reach of the lake, there would be another turn and then another and another. All the time the slopes alongside the water would get steeper and higher. Along the way they would have camped some more and it wouldn't have been so easy, since there are places where the shores are cliffs that drop without break into the water. It would be good to have sturdy canoes since it would be necessary to push on in spite of wind and rough water. And so in time they would come to the end and would beach their craft and walk.

Lake Chelan is a dramatic piece of water. It lies in a trench dug by a prehistoric glacier seventy-five miles long. The glacier receded after it had cut its hole in the range; water filled the bottom of the hole, covering the deepest part fifteen hundred feet. Peaks alongside the upper end of the lake rise more than six thousand feet above the water. The distance from shore to shore is about a mile and sometimes less than that. To get a sense of what this means, you have to stand on top of one of the ridges alongside the lake and look down. It is an awesome experience. A fair-sized boat on the lake shows up only as an invisible point at the head of the vee of its bow wave. The Indians wouldn't have shown up at all.

After the glacier retreated and the lake formed, the plug at the lower end wore down and some of the water went out. This shortened the lake by ten miles and at the upper end added a level valley to the gorge cut by the glacier and deepened by a river. Upstream, beyond the level part of the valley the Indians had a nice puzzle to solve, for there was a choice of converging valleys. If they took the one that looked easiest and most attractive, they were in trouble: it led to a high wall of peaks with glaciers hanging over their heads. If the Indians turned another way, they had to climb over a high ridge only to wind up on the eastern plains again. But there were a couple of valleys that headed into high passes which could be managed and beyond which they would be in the middle of the deep westside forests. These were routes, but only barely; trails were either faint or non-existent. The name was largely based on an illusion, then.

A small expedition was sent in by the Army once with the idea that a road across the mountains here would help control the Indians. The report made by the leader of that party said that the Army should forget about the matter; if the Indians needed controlling, there had to be better ways. And so, except for a wholly mythical wagon-road across one of the meaner passes, there has never been a road put through this area. Not that a road couldn't be made here—roads can be built anywhere and they usually are. This just happened to be a more than normally difficult—and luckier—area.

In strict truth, however, it has to be said that in time a road did get built in Stehekin—or maybe "developed" is a better term. It starts near the upper end of Lake Chelan, where the lake is still deep enough to allow boats to tie alongside the shore, and heads up the valley. In summer the road is a delight. After leaving the lake, it runs off through the woods more or less parallel to the river, avoiding trees that are too much work to cut, crosses the river twice, ducks under a waterfall, then hugs the edge of the river on a ledge a few feet above normal high water. It climbs to cross a wild tributary of the river and, after having found the main stream again, enters at last the great canyon of the upper valley, and as the grass and clover between the wheel tracks grow more luxuriant and the vine maple arches overhead, somewhere it ends. This may be twenty miles from the beginning—or seventeen, or twelve, or anything in between. Where it stops varies from year to year, and often more frequently. The end of the road may be a big log, a mass of granite fallen from the cliffs, or a long gap where high water has simply removed it. It is not an engineering marvel and it offers neither impulse nor opportunity for speed. Even when it extends over its maximum distance, however, a reasonably determined driver can expect to travel its entirety in less than three hours. Despite this flexibility of length, it has a quality of perfection: it is complete, whole in itself and unconnected with other roads. It goes nowhere because to do otherwise would be pointless.

The way such a road comes into being can still be seen in the one spur of any length that takes off from the main trunk in the valley. This track drifts off for three miles on the opposite side of the river before it ends. Long unrecognized by any public authority, it shows the process of road development. Someone possessed of the devil points the wheels of a car or truck into the woods, maybe along the general route of an old trail. He threads through the trees until he is stopped. If the obstacle is a rock and he has a shovel, he removes it and goes on. Sooner or later, of course, disaster strikes and the game is over for the time. But memories fade and madness strikes again, perhaps with a different driver, and the track goes farther. Each year a few more rocks are loosened and pushed to the side. It's a process of natural growth and —within limits—it's suited to the country.

The valley, like its road and its river, is a unity. It is separated from the rest of the world by concentric walls of rock, walls that are broken only by the lake that once was a way through. For a time, the lake was an avenue. In the eighteen nineties enterprise took hold at the foot of the lake and a steamboat was put into the water. After a few years it was left to rot on the beach, and a newer and grander sternwheeler took its place for a while before it sank and had to be raised and rebuilt. Something has always seemed to happen to the boats on Lake Chelan—fire, freeze-up, holes in the bottom and whatever else can happen to a boat. Perhaps there are special difficulties here; part of the trouble is being too far away from the sea and a nautical tradition. Fortunately the lake is narrow enough that navigation is not a problem, and no boat has been lost for any extended time in the sense of its skipper not knowing where he was, however unpleasant his whereabouts might be for a while.

There was a period—it might be called the lake's grand epoch—when the wood-burning steamboats got finer and finer. They were really big, considering the extent of their land-locked water, and they had staterooms and other touches of elegance. Passengers would take all of one day meandering up the lake, wait while wood that had been cut and stacked along the shore got loaded aboard, sleep for the night while the boat was tied up, and then go on the next day to their destinations uplake. Having got this far, more likely than not they would stay for days or even weeks at one of the two resort hotels, which catered to a moneyed and fashionable clientele. Although a few of the visitors might stray into the hills around, their interest focused on the lake and its swift-changing moods.

But this clientele proved fickle. As fashion shifted and Americans lost faith in any other than a single form of transportation, the arts of elegant living were lost and the sumptuous boats were abandoned. Their successors grew humbler through the years. Most of them were built elsewhere in places still having the craftsmanship of marine construction. In time, however, the vicissitudes of alpine navigation took their toll; and gradually, with the never-ending repairs of rough-and-ready carpenters, the boats all acquired a home-made air like the cabins and shacks of the hills around. Somehow it was more appropriate.

The firm that operated these craft persisted through the years, even when the public was turning its back on slow-paced water travel. It provided a service to the few people who for reasons of their own had allowed themselves to be beached and left uplake. Between the firm and these residents there developed a love/hate relationship. The boat company would overcharge and misdirect goods, its boat would come late or not at all, its crew would get arrogant and rude and local people would fume. And the local people would fail to pay their bills, deny having received things put ashore for them, and lose all tolerance for the problems the company had to contend with. At times it would seem that the breach was irreparable. But each side was dependent on the other and when some resident was down to no cash at all, the boat company would continue to carry his goods indefinitely. And at those critical moments when the license of the company was up for review and there were the inevitable questions about its monopoly, the residents would turn out in force and save the company's neck. So, annually at least, treaties of peace were made.

It went like this: The boat company would haul stuff uplake all year for somebody—Lew Weaver, say. Sometimes they would send along a penciled bill, but usually it would be forgotten and Lew would simply pick up what he knew he had coming uplake and take it home the way everybody did. The Tuttle brothers, who ran the company, might or might not send a bill after a few months, but Lew wouldn't bother to reply so there wasn't much use in sending the bills. At the end of the year, one of the Tuttles would come uplake and put in at the Weavers'. He would have a cigar box of notes on the loads the boat had brought them. Daisy, Lew's wife, would make some coffee and get out a cake. Then for a couple of hours a process of arguing and bargaining over each item would go on. At times this took on an Oriental quality. Once, for example, there was a deadlock on a note about "Two buggy wheels: 200 pounds." Both sides, of course, knew that nothing was ever weighed before it was put on the boat, estimate being made simply by a glance from one of the Tuttles, a factor that gave considerable leeway for bargaining. This time, however, Daisy was outraged. She went out to the shed, got the wheels and held them at arms length, one in each hand.

"Cap," she said, "Do you really think I can hold 200 pounds like this?"

A laugh settled the matter and they went on to the next item. In the end, Lew paid up in full and Daisy served dinner.

Perhaps it was a mistake to view the boat company as a business. It was poised somehow between two worlds, uplake and downlake, just as its craft were when they slowly traced the fifty miles between the two. At times the firm would seem to belong more to one, then to the other. And it varied with the different operators. The Tuttles certainly were the most perplexed by the problem, but they could never be accused of simply running a business.

There was the affair of Hubbard's pump, for example. Hubbard had come from the east and somehow never managed to forget it. He was formal and businesslike. His enterprise was successful—one of those two hotels along the lake, a place well known as being restful and decorous. Since it was located on a little spit of land built up where a steep side stream emptied into the lake, it was entirely isolated. As a result, Hubbard's rule of the establishment lacked any of the tempering influences from the presence of neighbors he might have had if he had been situated all the way at the head of the lake. All the same, he was just as dependent on the boat company as others along the lake.

Hubbard ordered a pump one day, an elaborate and modern pump that could only be had from Philadelphia. After several months the pump had not arrived, so he asked the boat boys if they had seen it. They shook their heads and he wrote back to Philadelphia. The answer was that the pump had long since been shipped. Hubbard then began a series of inquiries which resulted in a chain of confirmations that the pump had passed from one carrier to another across the continent and had reached the railhead for Chelan. And then at long last he held in his hand a crucial bit of paper bearing the Tuttle signature of receipt for the pump. Controlling his fury, he marched into the presence of the brothers at their dockside office and held out the damning evidence.

The Tuttles took one glance at the paper and burst into loud laughter.

"We were wondering how long you were going to take tracing that pump! It got here months ago. It dropped into the water while we were trying to load it. And we couldn't ever find it in all that mud."

They guffawed some more and then, still grinning, they paid the speechless Hubbard for the value of the pump.

*   *   *

On a cold, dark December day the boat brought us, its only passengers, uplake. There were just two of us, Jane and myself. According to the custom of the time, we were married, and we were headed for the first home we were to own, a small cabin in the Stehekin Valley. Why there? Well, why anywhere? Our lives had been uprooted by the war, our goods were in storage, and I had just received my manumission from the military. We had to go somewhere, and so, being momentarily gifted with freedom of choice, we decided to make a rational decision. Where would we most like to be? In the mountains. Which mountains? This was a more complex matter, but a pleasant one involving thoughts of areas we knew in different parts of the West; it softened a good many bitter hours in the years of tumult. After savoring a number of the possibilities, we narrowed their number; elimination led to Stehekin.

Perhaps this sounds like an unduly narrow basis of judgment. There were indeed a few hours while we were aboard the boat and thoroughly committed when I questioned it myself. We were belowdecks and out of the weather, but it was cold regardless. We were prepared for this, but then we saw that the usually arid hills near the foot of the lake had snow, more than I liked at the moment. The cargo area of the boat held our groceries and other supplies for the winter, and as I went back to gaze at the heap they made, I thought of the distance from the Stehekin dock to our cabin—seven miles, all the way to the end of that little spur road, certainly the part least likely to have been traveled recently. Obviously all my time and energy were going to be spent backpacking the stuff up on skis. And if that were so, when was I going to cut the wood we were going to need?

Our plan, such as it was, was that we should arrive ahead of the snow and induce somebody in the valley to haul our groceries up by truck. Viewed from New York, this had seemed thoroughly reasonable, since there are few places in the United States where snow comes in any great quantity much before Christmas. In any event, our departure date was not of our choosing; we simply came as soon as we could. Looking out at the shore from the boat, however, I could see the snow was deeper with each mile the lake penetrated into the mountains. And the cloud that hung in the lake's canyon drifted lower and lower at each bend. We were traveling in a dark tunnel that bore no resemblance to the sparkling mountain lake we had known in summer. The soaring granite cliffs that had led our eyes previously up to glittering peaks now simply dissolved into grey murk a few hundred feet above our heads. It was both forbidding and depressing. At last even this degree of visibility ended in a heavy fall of snow.

We were unprepared and unskilled for what we were about. We knew a bit about the high country above Stehekin, but that was in summer and we knew little about the valley itself at all. There's an after-the-fact self defense of sorts: any preparation we might have made would probably have been useless; the skills we might have acquired would have best been learned by doing what we were doing—coming to Stehekin. We weren't engaged in any great mission and had nothing in particular to prove.

As the motors cut and the dock emerged into sight, however, immediate and headlong retreat seemed the probable outcome. A few figures of vaguely human outline had approached the boat as it tied up and were quickly engaged in piling our goods in the snow. We headed for the little post office on the hillside to warm up. As we waited for the little cluster of people, perhaps five or six, to move away from the post office window, I saw the boat pull out and disappear in the falling snow; it wouldn't be back for two days. I wondered vaguely which of the strangers in the room I should accost and, more, just what I should say. Whatever it was, there wasn't any really good way of putting it. Suddenly, a familiar voice addressed us:

"Hey, are you two ready to go?"

It was Curt Courtney, from whom we had bought our cabin the previous summer. He lived with his family a half mile down the valley from us.

"Curt!" I practically yelled. "What do you mean, go? Isn't the road closed?"

"Well," he replied, "not *quite.* Come on; your stuff's on the truck and Laurence is waiting."

Laurence was Curt's brother and, like Curt, tall and powerful of build. We made things very tight inside the cab when we all got in and managed to slam the door. What ensued was something marvelous. Laurence headed the truck up the barely visible road and kept it going through snow that deepened markedly as soon as we left the lake. Before long we were going through snow that was more than a foot deep, and new snow was rapidly filling the two faint ruts. Several times we almost ground to a stop. The muscles in the side of Laurence's face tightened at those moments, and I thought I could feel a flow of will going directly from Laurence to the rear axle of the ancient vehicle. Gradually we picked up momentum again. Even so, it took more than an hour before we reached the old log cabin of the Courtneys. The truck stopped and I stepped out into nearly two feet of snow.

Mrs. Courtney came out of the door and down the shoveled path to greet us, and put her arms around Jane as soon as she was out of the cab. In the few weeks we had been in the valley the previous summer, we had hardly known her. She was shy to a point of embarrassment, but she had obviously liked Jane. Still, this was different. We started to go inside, for the air was cold.

"No," Mrs. Courtney said, "You go on and get yourselves settled. We'll have lots of time to talk."

I looked at Laurence questioningly, for what lay beyond was no road at all, as I well knew from the summer. He nodded and headed back to the truck. And indeed the tracks in the snow continued. It turned out that whenever the snow started, he had simply got into the truck and driven up to our place to mash the snow down. Sheer persistence had kept it an open route. All the same this last half mile took longer than I could have walked it even with the snow. Suddenly we were at the cabin, strangely different than we had remembered and much more handsome with the snow cover. And smoke was coming from the chimney.

A figure was standing in the door waving. It was Hugh, father of Curt and Laurence.

"Welcome home," he called. "I was pretty sure this was the day you'd make it."

Hugh, like his sons, was tall and, although in his sixties, vigorous and strong. Years before he had taken up a homestead in the valley and it was a corner of this, part of Curt's deeded share, that we had bought. On the last few boat days Hugh had been coming up to the cabin to build a fire on the chance it might be the day we would arrive. The house was warm and, although mightily crowded by the time we got all the goods piled up inside, comfortable to a degree I had not imagined. The Courtneys stayed a few minutes and went back in the truck.

This was the beginning of what we thought would be a winter. It turned out to be a period of years. It's difficult to reconstruct just what we expected beforehand, but the truth is probably that we expected very little of what we actually experienced. Probably there was some stereotype of discomfort and mild hardship, although both of us had been in the mountains enough not to imagine life there as necessitating any particular powers of endurance or fortitude. So far as such matters are concerned, my chief memory of the reality is of a sense of incredible luxury. This wasn't the luxury of an abundance of costly things about, of course—we had neither running water nor electricity—but we had a degree of freedom that seems to have been driven from the world. There were many symbols of this: a lack of fences—all the way into Canada, so far as I could tell—unlocked doors, and others. The most important, however, was freedom from measuring time by much else than the sun's movement and the onset of hunger. This began to dawn on me when I discovered that our clock was unreliable as a result of my frequently forgetting to wind it and setting it by guess. A sense of obligation told me that I ought to develop an automatic routine for winding it, but this was obviously hopeless when the calendar became untrustworthy. It was only about two weeks before neither of us knew what day of the week it was, and when we took this in, the sense of emancipation was delicious and almost physical.

For sheer animal comfort, however, nothing was more important than the wood-burning kitchen range. If the historians of technology have any sense, I am convinced they will one day record that civilization peaked out with the full development of the wood range. In its finest form this is probably the most sensitive instrument fashioned by man. Deceptively simple, like all great inventions, it contained fire—one of the elements in the ancient and most humanly important sense—and yielded its control through a minimum of levers and knobs so that an infinite gradation of warmth was possible. Within a few minutes of lighting a properly laid fire, a range could flood a room with heat when one came in from a cold day, or it could simply provide the soft low warmth hour after hour needed to work the yeast in bread rising on top of the warming oven. Someplace on top of the big flat cooking surface, one could find exactly the right temperature for every form of cookery; while meantime things could be going on in the oven, and plates would come warm just to the right degree from the warming oven. But food and warmth weren't the end of its offerings. In the evening, after the dishes were done with water from the big teakettle on its surface, the range would murmur companionably, responding to the mood of the hour, just as it had in a livelier and more snapping manner at the beginning of the day. It spoke of life itself with all its change of rhythms.

For these gifts, of course, there was a price. The first part was that management of the range had to be learned. A stranger experienced with a variety of wood ranges could walk into a house having a range he had never seen and get it to perform adequately. But only luck would allow a total novice to get it to work at all. Treated insensitively the range could retaliate unmercifully, either refusing to tolerate the burning of a match or producing sufficient clouds of smoke to drive the offender out into the open air. Or it could sulk, keeping just enough fire going to exhaust the culprit's patience but not enough to warm his hands. The real delights of living with such a range were available only to someone who had the time and opportunity to learn its personality and quirks. Each range was an individual to be treated with full respect.

The other part of the price was a supply of wood. I am prepared to insist that taking the trouble to learn to know one's range properly is a worthy enterprise in itself, good for the soul and acculturating to a way of life. Getting wood, however, is a reminder of original sin. This takes effort, large amounts of it. It requires strength, persistence and skill; it abrades the skin and wearies both body and spirit. Done in small stints, it can indeed yield a feeling of virtue rather like taking a quick dip in a glacier-fed stream on a sunny day. Getting a full winter's supply is another story.

By the time we had finished supper and done the dishes, we were in such a state of euphoria that not even the problem of the wood seemed serious. And to banish this from our consciousness, we walked to the Courtneys for our ceremonial call. We were not allowed to thank for our rescue and stayed longer than we had intended, mostly listening to stories from Hugh. As we got up to go, Curt asked,

"Say, when were you planning to get your wood?"

"As soon as possible, I guess."

"Well, we don't have ours in yet. Why don't we work together?"

I looked at Curt's massive frame. I thought of his truck. And I thought of my recent months of physical inactivity. It was absurd and magnificent. But best of all it was utterly unrefusable.

We began the next day. Curt had spotted a big dead fir several hundred yards below the Courtney place and we set to work with a long two-man cross-cut saw to fell it. This is the tool which destroyed a major part of the nation's forests, but the thought of this still staggers me. Not knowing Curt very well, I was determined to do my part or drop in my tracks. Which is precisely what I did on the first pull. Curt's arms were not much less than a foot longer than mine. This adjusted for in our pulls, however, we went on until the tree went down with a fine thundering crash. As it was now snowing again, we suspended operations for the day—barely in time for me. When I joined Curt the next day, the tree had disappeared beneath the night's fall of snow, and it took some time to locate it and clear it enough to get the old Courtney dragsaw into place on it.

As soon as the first block came free, I seized an axe—a thirty-six-inch-handled, double-bitted model—took careful aim, and sank the head precisely where I had intended, the very center of the block. My second try—after I had spent two or three minutes getting the bit out—was a rather poorer thing, three inches off center. The third was wild. None had had the slightest effect. At that point, Curt, who had stopped to watch, asked very mildly,

"Don't you always find that it splits best when you start at the edge?"

It had the air of professional consultation: we might have been two doctors weighing surgical technique. I started to respond in spirit, giving my own considered opinion—and stopped. A few tries following the advice were convincing.

It was a week before there was enough wood for the two houses. And the track to our woodshed stayed open just long enough to get our part hauled by the truck. It closed finally and categorically the next night. Sitting by the range next day my muscles and ego healed rapidly.

2.

The really heavy snow came in a series of storms that began with the closing of the road. Instead of an inch or two at a time, it came by feet. Through late December and all of January there were few breaks between storms and most were brief. During these breaks, bits of cloud would rush over the valley from one ridge to the other and be gone in five minutes. The violence of the winter was obvious, but even at such moments the air in the valley was still. In an hour or less the clouds would thicken and some would sink into the valley, and the snow would begin again. The track of the big storms was remarkably consistent and almost directly athwart the valley axis. The complete lack of wind inside the valley during winter produced an effect unusual where snow is heavy: since the snow fell vertically and was undisturbed by drifting, the outlines of rocks and logs on the ground were preserved even under many feet of snow. But even more impressive was the sense of quiet and seclusion that deepened apace with the snow.

This sense, which so far had seemed to be simply a product of the contraction of our environment to a few dozen feet in any direction, suddenly reached a climax when, for two days, the snow stopped and the clouds disappeared. It began one morning in early January. The dawn, which had been missing since our arrival, shone on the eastern ridge and then dropped into the valley, where it lingered. For several minutes the edge of the ridge was incandescent before the sun itself appeared. The ridge had never seemed particularly remarkable; it was simply one of the valley's walls. Despite a few cliffs on its side, there were trees on its crest and it was notably lower than most of the peaks of the area. Suddenly it was a mountain in its own right.

The same thing happened to the other ridges. But the transformation was greatest with the peak that rises at the head of the inhabited part of the valley, the lowest ten miles. By normal tests of steepness and height above its base it deserves the title of mountain in any season. Its rise is not much less than seven thousand feet in a horizontal distance of less than two miles. The summit cliffs culminate in a sharp point as seen from the valley, and the reverse side holds a small glacier. In summer and fall, however, most and occasionally all of its visible snow melts; at such times what seems most conspicuous about the mountain is its massive tree-covered base. Then it often seems from the valley that a higher peak should be supported by the base. This illusion is caused by a combination of the trees, which disguise substantial cliffs, and foreshortening. As the break in the winter storms came, however, the mountain stood forth as a coherent entity with no break between base and peak—and high, incredibly high.

This was McGregor. It's officially McGregor Mountain on the maps that give trails and so on, but probably nobody in the valley would know without looking at one of these maps whether it is this or Mt. McGregor; to the valley, it's simply McGregor. Whether this implies personification in anybody's mind, I don't know. It well could; such things happen in other places. In a world contracted to a few miles of the valley and its walls, McGregor when it emerges from the clouds is the dominating feature. A glance toward its summit is always in order when the weather is in doubt. As with any oracle, of course, its prophecies are often ambiguous. But it is reasonably certain there will be no immediate storm until clouds gather around its peak. Its other signs are more subtle and require both study and long experience to interpret. This useful service, however, is a small part of its hold on everyone who spends any time in the valley.

For a time I speculated about the name. McGregor, the human, should have been a hero of legendary stature to deserve such an honor. The facts, so far as they go, however, are disappointing. In the early days of the century Jack Blankenship went out to make a first land survey of the valley. He established one of his fixed points on a large boulder that lay in a level part. This was near the shack of an old fellow about whom all that is known is that he lived in the

29

shack, had been there for some time, and was named McGregor; nobody can even remember his first name. But the area around his shack was known as McGregor Flat (or was it then McGregor's Flat?). As Jack sought a second fixed point, he selected the big peak above the valley and wrote it down in his notes as McGregor Mountain. And so it became in print when the Forest Service issued its map.

At any rate this is a better state of affairs than usually happens with prominent peaks; surveyors normally leap to flatter their bureaucratic superiors with intimations of immortality by giving their names to such points. Even the world's highest mountain has not been spared this. In the Stehekin watershed the highest unnamed peak was thus named for a bureau chieftain named Goode. Local people, however, have taken unwitting revenge on his memory; they pronounce the name "Goodie."

Secure within the valley walls and watched over by McGregor, our lives settled into an uncontrived routine of great simplicity. This would have been even simpler had there not been that necessity of learning the elementary skills that were once the heritage of every family. If wood cutting was my first lesson in humility, bread making was Jane's. As the few loaves of store bread we had brought in disappeared, we both looked forward to the first homemade bread. This had a symbolic importance, not quite a declaration of independence from downlake, but smacking of it. The importance of the undertaking I could see was making Jane apprehensive, although she was normally not troubled by unfamiliar rituals. As supportively as possible, I assured her this was a simple process of following a recipe; many people had managed successfully before her. Making an exception to our already established rule of no fixed points of time, she set aside a day for bread making. Feeling the tension within her growing, I reminded her that her education was much more practical than mine—she had been through a graduate program in nursing—and she could certainly do it. Her manner, however, indicated that if our actual survival was not at stake, her status and self-respect were.

As she set to work things indeed seemed to go smoothly and I relaxed. I heard things being measured, sifted and stirred—then a long silence. Finally, she asked,

"What does it mean, 'to knead'?"

"What?"

"What does 'to knead' mean?"

"Are you serious?"

"Yes, just what do you *do*?"

"Well, you know, . . . *knead.*"

I went to the kitchen and looked at the situation. She had a big white blob sitting on the table. I looked at the directions, read them aloud and came to the instruction: "knead until mixture is smooth, elastic to touch, and bubbles may be seen under the surface." I tried poking the blob. It wasn't elastic and I couldn't see any bubbles. This was a reality problem after all. We sat down and had some coffee.

Suddenly inspired, I jumped up and went to the pile of books. We had a Webster's Collegiate Dictionary. Delightedly I turned to "knead" and then read, "knead (nēd), v.t. To work and press into a mass, as dough, usually with the hands." I also learned the word was from the Anglo-Saxon. I sat down again.

All at once Jane's face lit up. She left her chair and seized the blob.

"Hey," I asked, "what are you doing?"

"I know, I know. In one of my nursing courses they taught us how to give somebody a back massage. And the instructor told us, 'act as though you were kneading bread'."

The blob was forthwith flipped onto its stomach and kneaded. The process was on the violent side, I thought, but I had no intention of interfering. The result was excellent. Nevertheless, I hate to think of the tenuous thread that will have to be followed back to the basic original skills when contemporary technological civilization finally collapses.

Fortunately for us there was an ultimate recourse conveniently available: the Courtneys. We called on them regularly—to get milk, to ask advice, and more and more, just to talk. The family was a closely knit unit, with two adult sons on hand, and all three men paying deep tribute to Mrs. Courtney. Probably the moment when we felt we had really been accepted into the valley was when Jane was told we should use Mrs. Courtney's first name, Mamie. With Hugh, we had been on a first-name basis from the start and it seemed natural; this, however, was an honor and a very subtle one.

One day a few weeks after our arrival we found the Courtneys in a great state of excitement. They had just received a letter announcing the early return of Ray, the third son. Politely we listened to accounts of Ray from each member of the family. Ray was the youngest of the family, the handsomest, the brightest—there was no limit to the praise of him. He was obviously the young Joseph of the family. Unlike Curt or Laurence, he had persevered through school, even going downlake (the ultimate mark of devotion to learning) in order to attend high school. His record there had been superior in every way, from scholastic marks to winning a Golden Gloves championship (a competition he had entered to be sure he could defend himself). He was given to taking off into the woods with a knife and a few matches and surviving for weeks. He borrowed books from the Smithsonian Institution on anthropology, and he could argue anybody down. And now he was returning from the war.

The buildup would have been completely prejudicial if it had not been so thoroughly sincere. And when Ray finally arrived this was even more remarkable, for he was very different from Laurence or Curt. Taller than his brothers, Ray was as articulate as Curt and, without being silent like Laurence, quiet on the whole. But his great point of difference was in his view of the world. He had no time or respect for machinery, the passion of the other two. His aim at every point was to act and live harmoniously with the woods around him, using the simplest tools and giving respect to all the things of nature. This was long before the message of ecology became popular, and it would be good to think his outlook derived simply from having grown up in the valley. But there was opposite evidence of the valley's influence on Curt and Laurence. Their conclusion from the same upbringing was to devise and use mechanical aids whenever possible.

Ray had a considerable reserve, and we were slow in getting to know him. Accordingly, a week or so after his return we were surprised when he came up to our cabin as we were finishing breakfast. He joined us for a cup of coffee and we chatted for a while. Then he got up and went to the door. He held it open for a couple of minutes, looked out at the snow that was still coming down and asked,

"By the way, how would you like to give a party?"

"Well, uh," Jane replied, "why sure."

Ray still stood in the doorway, and we waited for him to go on. He remained silent. Then Jane said,

"We're not exactly organized yet, but yes, let's have a party. Who should we ask?"

"Oh, there's Beryl, the Buckner girls and, well, I don't exactly know who all."

It still seemed a startling idea, but a good one all the same. There would be a lot to do to straighten the place out, things like getting the cartons of groceries in the main room stashed somewhere so people wouldn't fall over them and so on.

"When should we give the party?" Jane asked.

Ray shuffled his feet and looked uncomfortable.

"Well," he said, "they're on their way up right now."

He started to close the door and put on his hat.

"Wait! You mean we're to give the party today?"

"Yes, Beryl phoned up about an hour ago. They were about ready to start."

"Uhhh... And how many of them are on their way?"

"I didn't find out, maybe ten or twelve."

He made his escape in the silence that followed.

And so we gave a party. Or perhaps it would be better to say that a party occurred. There were indeed a dozen who skied up to our place, a majority of the people then in the valley. At first it seemed that the principle of selection was age—on the whole, the group that came consisted of the valley youth. But this was not correct; the principle was ideology. The valley was split on the issue of skis versus snowshoes. One was either willing to use skis or not. There was really no compromise on this. In the deep loose snow of a Stehekin winter a party of mixed snowshoers and skiers is

34

an impossibility; the tracks are incompatible and the paces are utterly different, the snowshoers being fast uphill and the skiers fast downhill. It would be good to be able to say that the partisans of each side were tolerant and willing to see that there were virtues to both modes of travel, but unfortunately this was not true. Debates on the matter were frequent, prolonged, loud and sterile. Each side looked down on the other and was not above relating the use of the other mode to deficiencies of character. And if a member of one camp had just had to contend with a trail messed up by a member of the opposite camp, there was likely to be a highly sarcastic exchange of remarks. It was just as well for valley peace that winter lasted no longer than it did.

Ours was a skiers' party, then, and skiing on the hill behind the cabin was the chief form of entertainment. That and eating. To our great relief the crowd brought food, quantities of it. Beryl took charge of the kitchen. One of the gifted cooks of the world, she also had rapport with our range. She could adjust the fire and tune the range to such a fine point that it sang. And the results were prodigious. I found my main function to be supplier of wood to the kitchen and fireplace. In this, however, I was joined by Bert, a visitor from downlake who was staying for a few days at Buckner's. He was husky and willing to work but thoroughly unskilled, so I took pleasure in teaching him how to use an axe, a pleasure mitigated by his breaking the axe handle. I couldn't hold this against him, however, since he did so much for my self esteem. After building up the fireplace fire to the point where it almost set the house alight, he explained how things were done in Chicago, his home. Instead of a fireplace or a little stove like we had in the kitchen, the people in Chicago had concrete-lined holes under their houses, where they put really big stoves that sent heat through pipes all over their houses so that every part was warm. I indicated this sounded impressive but that I doubted it was practical. At least *some-body* thought I fitted in to Stehekin.

The party went on for two days and nights at our cabin. Then, as the food that had been brought up was largely gone, it adjourned down the valley to the Buckner's. This was the other family, the only other, that is, in which the children remained in the valley. Since all three of the children were girls, the Buckner place was the social focus for the entire community. But this was not the whole of the explanation. It was a spot that radiated warmth and hospitality to a degree I have not seen matched. The head of the household, Harry, was a vigorous outgoing man with an enormous capacity for enjoying life, a quality he shared with his wife, Olive. As at the Courtneys', nearly everything was home-made; but since there was an orchard at Buckners a certain amount of cash came in and there were some important extras around the house—an abundance of books, for example. Because of the warmth of the household, the modestly greater degree of wealth, and the long presence of the family in the valley, its standing was clearly preeminent in the community. This was a fact of slight importance, except when there was some question on which local opinion was sought by a downlake power, the moguls of county government especially. Then it was Harry Buckner who was sought out and his became the voice of Stehekin.

There was a degree of resentment in the valley when Harry was thus deferred to, not because his responses were injudicious or self-serving, but simply because he was so consistently selected by downlakers. It was a resentment directed far more against downlake than against Harry since the deference implied an imputation of downlake values and downlake social distinctions to Stehekin. In this sense, the behavior of downlake was akin to that of British colonialists who expected always to find a local headman through whom their own rule could be imposed on any remote society they came across.

So far as valley matters were concerned—that is to say, in domestic as against foreign affairs—not even Harry could be regarded as a headman. The Stehekin population consisted strictly of co-equals. Authority, moreover, had never been yielded up to anyone, whether by contract or force of arms. It's a horrendous thought to imagine anyone trying to lead Daisy Weaver, for example. Since her husband's death years before, she had continued to live in a little shack at the end of the lake and across the river from the road. The only feasible way of reaching her place was by boat to the post office dock, a good mile. Since every freshet brought down quantities of trees with big root systems which caught in the shallow water, negotiating this mile was a very tricky thing. Daisy would come and go in almost any kind of weather, standing up in her little boat to pick a feasible route. She split her own wood and did everything about the place there was to be done, everything, that is, unless she captured an unwary guest who thought chivalry demanded his help with the heavy labor she always had lined up. When this happened, the guest was held to exacting and exhausting standards of performance, namely, those she met herself. Failure to keep up with her was likely to arouse her displeasure, a fate no one could desire. She found other reasons to be displeased, too, although these were not always obvious. In fact, it looked at times as though she simply laid her displeasure on one person after another on a rotational basis. A year or so after our arrival in the valley, she decided that she should be known and addressed as Weaver, plain and simple. Everyone complied, for reason of expediency if nothing else. So we were awed when one day she conferred on us the privilege of addressing her as Daisy. It was our second such honor, but very different in kind from the invitation given by Mamie Courtney. She would have made some sovereignty a great empress.

In one way or another everyone in the valley had a streak of fierce independence. Houses were scattered with so much distance between them that self-reliance was a necessity, but there was probably an element of choice in this distribution. The one place where several households lived in close proximity was at the dock and it was a notable fact that, although there were some changes in the inhabitants, friction was its persistent condition. It seemed to follow from all this that organized community activities were impossible. Had anyone undertaken to lead the valley people in some common venture—no matter how desirable—reasons would have been found for opposing it and nothing would have come of it.

And yet, there were community activities. Our party was an example. How it or any of the others came about was a mystery. But perhaps it was a mystery only in terms of the model that prevailed downlake, a model that was military at heart and held that everyone occupied some point in a rank order and that somebody was always in charge, even when this was not formally declared. In Stehekin most occasions of common effort arose from needs that were obvious to everyone in the valley and then the things to be done were equally obvious and no organization of command was needed, as when fire broke out or someone was injured in the woods. So it may have been that the explanation for our party was merely that enough time had gone by, and everyone felt a need for a party. And what finally moved the crowd down the valley was the disappearance of the food the others had brought with them; somehow our stocks didn't look very impressive with that number of people in the cabin. Anyhow, there was no place at our end of the valley for a square dance and Harry, the only caller in the valley, had not come. And it was with a dance that the affair concluded.

The real event, however, was winter itself. The party, trips to the neighbors' or the dock were distractions in a literal sense; they drew attention away from the main event, but only in part. We could be sitting in the Courtney cabin talking and laughing, yet it would still be impossible to keep from watching the snow piling up against the window. Mostly this was sheer fascination, but it was cautionary as well. There were occasions when the rate of fall was a foot an hour. Then it was wise not to stay too long. And if the snow stopped during the night, the morning news was written on the new surface in the form of tracks across it. Deciphering their meaning was not always easy, but the evidence was plain that we were not the only inhabitants.

January was a time of almost continual storm. Yet it was difficult to think of it as storm. A cloud hung in the valley and seemed scarcely to stir, even when occasional holes opened and the ridge of McGregor showed through. But the holes would close without any perceptible movement of air, and the snow would resume. Falling vertically, it seemed to move more slowly and more softly than elsewhere. It was light, filled with air, and built up in an impossible house-of-cards structure. Six hours or maybe a whole day would go by before the mass would collapse and settle down to a fraction of what it had been.

The paradox was that the time of the greatest storms was also the time of the greatest calm and quiet, or so it seemed. An undertone from the river is the normal condition of the valley. Over the course of a year this sound is not constant: it fluctuates with the seasons, rising in volume as the runoff comes in early summer and falling afterward as the snows of the high country vanish. In summer and fall it's also an index of events at the edge of the watershed: short, sharp, localized storms that bring one tributary or another to a momentary peak. After a lag of as much as six hours, there's a crescendo from the river for an hour or so as the crest passes down on its way to the lake. The river at such times is apt to be muddy and out of character, but the real announcement is sound. During spring and summer the sound frequently reaches the level of consciousness, but in late fall and winter it lies below the threshold and is felt in the same manner as one's own pulse—noticed only when it changes. But the river's changes in winter are slight and subtle. Since the flow of water then is at its lowest and fluctuations in it are rare, the changes of sound are simply degrees of muting by the fall of snow. And so, despite the quiet of a valley snowfall, its density can be gauged by ear.

As I stepped outdoors one late afternoon near the end of the third week of January, a strong sense of change struck me. The light was dim, and I could see only that snow was falling, as it had been all day. Perhaps a minute went by as I stood groping for what was different. The impression was strong but tantalizing; there was nothing to see, feel—or hear. But that was it, of course; there was silence, complete silence. The murmur of the river was as thoroughly gone as if the flow of water had stopped.

Total silence is not often experienced, and it had a curious effect, leaving me feeling that I should hold my breath and walk lightly. Unconsciously we lowered our voices at supper and talked less than usual. The ordinary sounds of the fire in the range and the movement of pots and plates seemed excessively loud. We sat by the table after supper, each of us pretending to read. I found myself watching the snow falling against the window, half of which was already covered. The level rose rapidly and it seemed as though I were caught in some unearthly situation where time was accelerated but emptied of meaning.

How long this actually went on is impossible to say—an hour or two perhaps. The silence was finally broken by a long heavy rumble so low in pitch it seemed to rise from the earth beneath us. We rushed to the door and threw it open. There was a second rumble, but this time fainter, as though it were an echo of the first. Yet the snow was falling more densely than ever, and the air was wholly lacking in resonance. We stood for a minute more and then a great prolonged crash roared out of the darkness toward us and the cabin shook with the impact of the sound. Almost instantly another crash came, this time farther away, then another nearby.

Every face of the valley walls was avalanching. Some of them we could imagine from having stared long at particular cliffs, but the roar was so nearly constant we knew that there were slopes we had never seen or given thought to, and it was hard to believe anything in the valley was immune to their threat. Yet reason told us we were safe, and mentally we constructed pictures of every home in the valley, one after another. Singly, each seemed safe (as indeed it turned out), but collectively all seemed doomed as though the breathless acceleration of the earlier evening had actually brought time to an end.

We sat listening for what may have been hours before the sound gradually diminished and became intermittent. The fire in the range went out unnoticed and the house grew cold. As we finally retreated to bed, it was with a sense that we had been witnesses to an absolute and were the last to remain.

3.

During the winter
and for most of the year,
the boat came three times a week.

There was also a possibility that it might come on
Sunday, but nobody could be sure of this. What
brought it in every Monday, Wednesday, and
Friday was the mail contract. Stehekin had a
third-class post office and Beryl was the postmaster (yes, post*master*). Considering that
Stehekin was inhabited by individuals who
cherished seclusion and isolation, the importance of the mail was astonishing. Going for the
mail was strenuous and, through the period of
deep snow, a protracted undertaking. And yet it

was something that had to be done and was always spoken of in tones reserved for deep obligation.

For a time I was strongly impressed by the sternness of this sense of duty toward the mail. As I reached for the full sense of it, I saw it as the sign of a profound humanity in the people who lived in the valley, a mark of fellowship with those unfortunate beings who dwelt outside. Going for the mail was thus a symbolic act, a kind of devotion. My appreciation for the local inhabitants rose sharply as this picture took shape in my mind, and I was not a little touched with awe. Behind these rough exteriors, and hidden by the caustic language with which they discussed all downlake things, were a delicacy of feeling and a perception of the oneness of the human condition that no philosopher of my reading had matched.

It is sad to record that this picture was almost wholly wrong. The truth was simply that Stehekinites loved to go for the mail. It was an excuse to get outside when nothing much else could be done outdoors, and it was the occasion for a three-times-a-week community meeting. Not that there was any community business. Indeed, the very idea that there might be any was an alien one that if ever suggested would have been indignantly rejected. The major topic of discussion was almost invariably local gossip. This was exchanged in full around the stove as everyone dried out from the long trip through the snow, and stored up for retailing to the family members who had not made it to the dock that day. Although the chain of rumor had only a few links, Stehekin gossip was not to be matched for unreliability. There wasn't anything vicious in this; it was merely that the neighbors delighted in stories, and the slender threads of fact spun at the dock became the warp on which the woof of elaboration was prepared during the long trip home. Our neighbors were not philosophers but poets.

If the post was markedly late, and it usually was—a fact so nearly consistent that the occasions when it came in on time were regarded as malicious trickery by the boat boys—the gossip was exhausted early and the discussion would turn to some problem of engineering. If somebody admitted to an intent of building a new barn or even a woodshed come summer, the assembled elders curtly dismissed any existing plans for it and hammered out a different and wholly novel one. In such arguments the prospective builder had rights equal but not superior to those of the others. I am sure that my own greatest contribution to the fellowship of the community was my innocent statement at one of those sessions that I hoped to introduce running water into our cabin in the spring. This carried the group through all of February and most of March.

There were, of course, other reasons for going to the dock. High on the list of these was entertainment, the delight of watching the occasional strangers who somehow found their way up the lake. A couple of these might have some kind of business (and of these it was best to be wary), but the others were simply tourists and so ridiculous that it was impossible to refrain from self-congratulation. And there might even be some mail. Certainly everyone waited until Beryl had distributed whatever had come in before departing. This was nine-tenths genuine obligation. Without the mail, the whole pretext would be gone and there would be no summons for the next meeting.

So, even though we did not yet fully understand the true nature of the obligation, Jane and I assumed our turn to go for the mail. During the depth of the winter this was a full day's venture. Of course there were times after big storms when one day was not enough. Then two or three of us from our end of the valley would start out on skis, each person breaking trail for a hundred yards before stepping aside panting while the next few hundred yards were broken. The return home from the halfway point would be rapid after three pairs of skis had packed the trail, and the next day would see the party all the way down to the dock and back. But this was not normal and, given a start by nine o'clock in the morning, Jane and I would be back not too much after dark the same evening.

The hours were by no means all spent in slogging along the trail. On the outgoing leg of the journey, the person going for the mail would have to stop along the way to receive commissions from neighbors; on the return trip he was obliged to deliver the incoming mail and report on doings in the valley. There was first of all the Courtneys, and since they were our closest neighbors and a full household, we would stop for coffee. This meant shedding skis and parkas. Then there were the Leshes. Old Frank might be out at the road to meet us with a letter, but at other times we would have to go off the route up to his house, and then it was more than likely that Mrs. Lesh was just taking bread out of the oven and this took more time and more coffee. At the bridge there was usually Skinny Wilson, who never went himself to the dock, but who nevertheless had to be filled in on doings on our side of the river before he snowshoed back to his house. By this time we were probably late and had to push if we were to catch Harry and his sled. If the snow was good, we made it; then there was the bliss of ski-joring behind as Harry clucked at the team to step along. On such days we made a very stylish arrival at the dock.

The return behind the sled as far as Buckner's was a beating of the game, for we went rapidly. But the time gained could all too readily be lost: an invitation to stay for dinner was easy to come by and if we weakened so much as to come in and get warm, there would be a very late arrival at our end of the valley. This would mean that Skinny would be kept standing at the bridge and rough going if snow was piling up in our morning's tracks. So we tended to be firm and push on. By the time the light from the Courtneys' Aladdin Lamp pierced the dark, we were willing enough to take off skis and go inside to make our report. And unless we were careful, this last pause could stretch out into an hour or two before we found the gumption to struggle on home. Once there, the cold threw us into a flurry of fire building, lighting lamps and shedding of wet outer clothes as the kitchen warmed. Unless our luck had been bad, as it was the day when the Sears Roebuck catalogues arrived (items unthinkable to leave behind), the day was one of utter satisfaction—friends encountered, a magnificent landscape traversed and duty performed.

So gradually we became acculturated. This came about unconsciously, through a process which we later came to understand. In retrospect, it took two forms. The first was simply participation in the necessary activities of the valley, like going for the mail or responding to some crisis. The other was what today I can only call instruction. We were taught—by Harry, by Hugh, by Hobbie, by Beryl, by Mamie, by Virgil and Rhoda, and most of all by Curt. There were very few residents of the valley, in fact, who did not at one time or another have a hand in our education. The teaching was very simple and straightforward where some skill was involved that we knew we lacked. How do you make cottage cheese from the skim milk the Courtneys gave us? Mamie was very clear. So was Hugh when I complained about the treacherous behavior of our Aladdin Lamp (sprinkle some salt on the mantle). There were many occasions when we went running to the neighbors for solutions that were not obvious, and even for some that should have been so. The lessons were given gladly and completely without addition to the embarrassment we initially felt in asking. It was only when we repeated questions that had once been answered that there was a gentle kidding. This hit me most frequently on matters relating to machinery (of which fortunately we had little).

There was instruction of a different kind, however, and it could be quite subtle. This occurred where the nature of valley relationships were most complex. On such matters we were often apt not to see at first that we were being instructed. This was partly due to our own denseness but more to the deep courtesy of the valley people. The simplest example of this courtesy was Curt's showing me how to split a big block of fir—my realization that I had been instructed was wholly a double take. That was also the occasion when I was first introduced to the valley's economic ethic.

Had anyone sought by questioning to learn the most important values of the valley, the answers would undoubtedly have been independence and self-reliance. I am certain that everyone believed this and in substantial part it was true. Why else come to so remote a spot as this? Everyone expected to keep his own house in repair, to get his own food and wood. No one expected to be a burden on the neighbors or to have to go running for help on things he should have done himself. And nobody wanted to be pushed around by anybody else, a feeling which was mutually respected, even between households that held less than affection for each other. The language in which this was expressed was almost straight out of nineteenth century Social Darwinism.

As Curt and I worked on that wood log during our first week of real Stehekin residence, he would call for breaks. We would rest on the log (I now think these stops were mainly for my benefit) and Curt would talk about the valley.

"What the valley needs is a welding outfit and a decent dragsaw. This one is shot."

It most certainly was; the engine was downright sick and the frame was split and loose. I agreed with him wholeheartedly after a few hours of wrestling with the thing. But the welding outfit?

"Who knows how to weld?"

"Oh, Laurence, Harry; I can do it."

"Isn't it expensive?"

"Well, not when you think of what you can do with it. Man, there've been times up here when having an outfit in the valley would have saved us two weeks or maybe more. Something breaks and by the time you get it down to the dock and send it downlake and they get around to doing what you have asked for, you've been shut down ten days easy. And when it does come back, it's probably not right."

The reasoning was strong; I already knew enough of dealings with downlake to have to agree. But who would own it and where would the money come from?

"You mean we'd all get together and chip in to buy a dragsaw and a welding outfit?"

"Lord no. You couldn't get anybody to do that. No, one person buys one thing and another person another thing and so on. The whole valley uses them."

"What if the fellow who bought one of the things doesn't want to lend it?"

"Well, I guess that happens, but anybody who acts that way isn't exactly popular. He just isn't part of the valley."

"What happens when one of these machines breaks down?"

"Why, the man who broke it fixes it."

"Suppose different people want to use something at the same time?"

"The person who needs it most gets it first."

As we went back to work it was obvious to me that I was operating on the basis Curt had outlined then and there. Cantankerous as the old Courtney dragsaw was, without it Jane and I wouldn't be getting in our wood. At home that evening we went through the Sears and Ward catalogues and found the latest in dragsaws. As financial manager, Jane was skeptical, but my knowing masculine eloquence won the day. We committed ourselves to buying a dragsaw as soon as the snow went off. And despite Jane's doubts, Curt got a welding outfit, a device whose presence ultimately benefitted us by keeping the dragsaw going.

Curt was right and he wasn't putting anything over on us. The concept of ownership in Stehekin had a very special quality. Whatever title that purchase gave had little to do with use. Need was the only valid claim for that. It had to be real need, however. At first I thought the hole in the scheme lay in the problem of determining need. Who would decide? Somehow, though, this wasn't a problem. In our case, Curt decided our needs. He knew we needed the help of his drag-saw—and also that we needed to have something of our own purchase to lend around the valley, a new dragsaw in particular. And he knew it before we did.

Control of the instruments of production, then—for the principle applied with special force to machines—lay in the people of the valley. And yet, there was a token given to the forms of capitalist ownership, not exactly a fiction, but then one not particularly reassuring to anyone with more conventional views of private property either. This lay primarily in the understanding that the owner of the item in question had custody of it, at least over the long term. It could be argued that this was more burden than privilege, since it involved keeping track of the item in its valley wanderings—not always an easy thing to do. The principle of need might require taking a tool or machine off one job and moving it to another without notification of the owner. Thus, at one point we assembled all of the five hydraulic jacks in the valley on an emergency basis when a project to straighten up a corner of the house foundations with a single jack threatened to bring the whole structure down; various other structures in the valley were left sitting on blocks of wood when we extracted jacks already in place. The owners, as in other cases, got their property back in time, but it *took* time.

Being inept and mistrustful of machinery, I used to wonder why anyone in the valley consented to be the owner of anything commonly useful. The answer was a mixture of considerations. First, there was the implicit obligation based on the fact of previous borrowings: you simply felt better if you occasionally loaned something to somebody who had loaned you something. Second, what you acquired was almost by definition something you couldn't borrow, i.e., something that was missing in the valley. Third was the joy you felt in getting out of a job that done by hand was drudgery. Drudgery—sheer physical backbreaking drudgery—is something which a surprising number of Americans have never encountered. But when one has had to cut five cords of mountain fir, or do any one of the heavy jobs that were conditions of survival in Stehekin, the idea of getting it done other than by hand and sheer sweat is enormously attractive. And this remained true when it occasionally became obvious that inducing the machinery to work could be even more laborious and frustrating. But of this, more later.

Whether or not this rational basis was fundamental to the Stehekinites' love of machinery, I could never be sure. I'm inclined to think that as time went on it receded far into the background, and that love went out to machinery for its own sake. Right after Curt got his first Cat—an obsolete gasoline-powered tractor the Forest Service got rid of simply by driving it into the shallow water at the end of the lake, and from which Curt promptly rescued it—I asked Curt why he wanted it. He was dumbfounded and stuttered for a minute.

"Why, man, think what you can do with it."

"What?"

More stutterings and then after quite a long pause, he gave a list of things; few of which, I'm sure, he had up to that moment thought of wanting to do. The tractor was simply a thing of yellow beauty.

Despite the heavily conventional character of valley ideology, the local economy was a far cry from anything resembling the ideal states posited by Adam Smith or Alfred Marshall. To begin with, the fundamental principle of the division of labor by which Smith set so much store was explicitly rejected in Stehekin. Every man and every woman was a Jack-of-all-trades. (That inclusion of women is no act of deference to feminism: there wasn't a woman in the valley who couldn't split wood; it was Daisy, not Curt, who taught me how to drive a tractor.) Everyone was expected to be able to do anything or at least to tackle anything. This was partly a matter of necessity. Nobody in the valley had the cash to hire real experts, and when such did occasionally visit the valley, their incapacity to make do with the tools and materials locally available was simply laughable. Getting along with substitutes on both scores was an essential talent for living in the valley, and only valley people seemed to have it.

This was part—but probably only a part—of the explanation for the makeshift quality of much of the work that got done in the valley. Almost nothing was highly machined, polished or nicely fitted. "Cobbled-up" was the valley term for the work to be found on almost anybody's place. For a long time I assumed the lack of materials, proper tools and skill to be the explanation for this: it was certainly adequate in my own case. And yet, valley skills were considerable and a sense of craftsmanship in many areas definitely existed. There was something beautiful, for example, in the way many of the valley people handled a double-bitted axe, whether in felling a tree on exactly the right line or notching a log for a cabin. And Ray's work with leather had genuine artistry, while Curt's cabinet work, at least what was done on his own time, was highly precise.

Something else was definitely involved, and this can only be described as a determined amateurism. There was actually a kind of pride taken in inexpert work. This was not the sort of amateurism associated with an aristocratic tradition, the kind that holds too great a degree of skill in anything as the telltale sign of lower class origins; but it was not wholly unlike it, either. Both shared a thinly disguised contempt for the ways of the wage-earning and commercial world. To work for wages or in any way go by the clock were marks of weakness, not least of all in character. The term "wage-slave" was one I never heard in the valley, but it expresses an idea that was common to almost everybody who lived in Stehekin. One might be forced to go to work for wages, but having a job was nothing to rejoice in. And to engage in such work beyond absolute need was crass and subhuman. Not to stop to chat pleasantly when a friend came by, to do only those jobs which paid best, to ignore the priorities of family or even the call of a fine day for fishing—these were stigmata of character appropriate perhaps to the downlake world, but unfit for Stehekin.

The incident of Harry's second woodshed illustrates the issue as well as anything else. Harry, being an eminently provident man, cut more wood one year than he could get into his woodshed. He stacked it close by and then, to keep the wood protected from rain and snow, laid some old boards across the top. In time he began to use the wood, and to protect the remainder, propped up the boards with four poles that were lying about. The wood eventually was all burned, but the boards remained propped in air. So, when he once again had a surplus of wood, he piled it under the makeshift roof. The thing continued in useful service for many years. It was a joke that everyone, especially Harry, enjoyed.

The theory of value that was operational in Stehekin was also a far cry from that beautiful structure built by classical economists. It was much closer, in fact, to the Marxist idea of use value. Yet it was not wholly unrelated to the facts of scarcity either. Thus, many of the necessities of life—a shake roof for example—had value directly related to the need for protection from the elements. But you could go out in the woods with a saw, an axe, and a froe, and get yourself some fine shakes. Sometimes the best cedars turned out to be located on Forest Service property and then a bit of negotiation or even less formal arrangements might be necessary, but the material was fundamentally there for the taking and investment of a bit of effort in it. (The labor theory of value had a certain relevance, too.)

It was other kinds of material that brought us to realize there were some subtle complexities in valley economic theory. This came about in our first spring just as the snow was going off. A little to the side of the track to the Courtneys'— even by Stehekin standards it couldn't be called a road—and partially hidden by a bit of buckbrush, we noticed some junk and debris poking out of the fast-melting snow. We went over and kicked at it. Several responses followed: first, disgust at the carelessness and messiness of whoever it was who had tossed the stuff there; it offended our budding ecological sense. Next, curiosity; it was a veritable kitchen midden and had an appeal that must be felt by an archeologist who has uncovered a pile of ancient artifacts. There were some old car batteries, aluminum pots, a Model T axle, bits of this and pieces of that. Almost all of it was metal. We kicked the snow away and pulled the heap apart. I made a mental note that there was some baling wire that could be untangled. Even the pots, decrepit as they were, might be cut up and used for something or other. Jane, meanwhile, was tugging at the pile and came up with what had evidently once been the oven rack of a kitchen range.

"What do you want with that?" I asked.

"I don't know. But it might come in handy some day."

And she carried it home.

A couple of days later Curt came up to the house on some errand, or more probably just to have a cup of coffee and chat. As he was leaving, his eye caught the oven rack. He picked it up and gave a twisted little smile, and asked,

"*Where* did you get this?"

"Why, we found it in an old dump by the road," Jane replied.

"What are you going to do with it?"

"Nothing I know of, but I thought it might be useful somehow."

"Well sir," Curt said slowly, "that's the rack from an old range the folks used to have. The range got burned out."

"Curt," Jane said a bit impatiently, "we found it tossed out there in the woods; it had been thrown away."

Curt put the rack down and came back inside and took a chair. It was plain that he had something to tell us. He grinned as he often did, but he was serious, really. We sensed that we had been caught red-handed in an act of theft. Curt explained himself very carefully.

"You see, I put that rack out there, and all that other junk, too. We used to have a junkpile way out in the woods back of the barn and we'd haul stuff to it by hand. It was out of the way and out of sight. But we found that we were always going out to get something or other and hauling it back. As Dad says, if you want something made of wood all you have to do is take an axe and go out and get the wood to make it out of.

But if you need something out of metal, it's a lot tougher. When we found we were always going out after the stuff we had thrown away, one day Laurence and I went out and hauled the stuff up to where you found it; it's a lot more convenient."

And Curt knew precisely what was in that pile. While he was willing to forgive us our sin, he did want us to know the real nature of our offense. What we had stolen was valuable, even though neither he nor we knew for what. It just might come in handy someday. For a while I thought I had grossly underestimated the respect given private property and that our failure to recognize his vested rights in that junkpile accounted for the stern tone of his lecture to us. But that wasn't it at all. No, the trouble was that not only did we have no need for the rack when we took it, we had assumed that what might someday come in handy for us might not also come in handy for somebody else. We were contrite as Curt disappeared down the path bearing the rack.

Had Stehekin resourcefulness continued or deepened over a sufficiently long period, it is thinkable that bits of copper and silver ore might have been picked out of the little outcroppings at the end of the valley and smelted into something useful. Iron and other metals, unfortunately, were to be found only in the form of rusty-colored hillsides, and in dumps like that one of Curt's. The latter represented a rational economic response to the problem of materials. There was, however, another kind of response, one that gave less of a role to rationality. It wasn't so much that the people of Stehekin were not rational as that it betrayed their deep-seated sense of the irrationality of the outside world.

One day in late October, when the broadleaf maples were

brilliant yellow like the larches on the high ridges and the vine maple was fiery red, a hunter came down to the dock and announced he had discovered the wreckage of an airplane. Since there had been no word of a missing plane, he was questioned a bit by the locals, who had had considerable experience with the alcoholic propensities of hunters suffering from the chill of their chosen season. Finally, someone went up the valley to High Bridge and plunged off into the dense brush of the area the hunter had indicated. Sure enough, there was wreckage from a plane crash spread over a square mile. Since brush was growing up through the debris, it was obvious the disaster had occurred some years before. Dutifully, a report was passed down the lake to the Sheriff. A day or so later, a message was radioed up over the Forest Service equipment from the United States Navy:

"Rope area of plane crash off, keep crowd at distance."

Even without the rope, the crowd kept at a distance— twelve miles, in fact. In another couple of days a task force of naval landing craft appeared at Stehekin and disgorged trucks and men who proceeded to the site of the crash. The sailors removed a couple of armloads of battered electronic gear and disappeared down the lake. But before they went, somebody asked the Commanding Officer if it was all right to let the crowd in. The only answer was a terse, "Yeah."

So the first crowd moved in, probably Harry. Then other crowds came and each one bore off pieces of the airplane. Fortunately, the crash, which had taken place during an early winter of the war, had involved no fatalities, the crew having bailed out successfully when the plane got lost on the west side of the range, so there was no prospect of unpleasant discoveries. Gradually in the course of the next few years each household in the valley came to have a stockpile of blue-painted aluminum. Its use was limited only by necessity and individual imagination. Most of ours was installed in the plumbing system, used as roof flashing or fashioned into cookie sheets. But, as in other places in the valley, there is a heap of the stuff out behind the woodshed; it will come in handy some day. That airplane was simply an unusually dramatic example of the queer ways of the downlake world. But when in its insanity it chose to drop something of value on Stehekin, none of us were so foolish as to ignore a windfall.

Obviously, the conventional downlake measure of value—money—played a somewhat different role in Stehekin than it did elsewhere. In the first place, there wasn't very much of it. Stehekinites tended to do without it or, at any rate, to rely a good deal of the time on other means of exchange and obligation. Once at the lunch counter a tourist pulled out a twenty dollar bill and offered it in payment for a hamburger. Beryl looked at the man and just before she exploded, Harry, seated a couple of stools away, explained,

"If you got that bill changed here, you'd stop circulation in the valley."

This was perfectly true, but it wasn't just a matter of poverty. The allocation of materials, labor and commodities in the valley depended much more on principles other than ability to pay. The clearest illustration of this was the few people who depended on purchase for their winter's wood. One case was a family who had come in to attempt to operate the old hotel at the dock. The cash flow of this enterprise was substantial and for a time it was even profitable. The other household needing to buy wood was that of an elderly widow who had been long in the valley. Curt and Laurence were the primary source of wood-cutting labor, however much they grumbled about it. Early after their arrival, the new hotel keepers offered to buy wood and indicated willingness to pay any near-reasonable price. The widow on the other hand was accustomed to paying only the same amount that she had spent many years before, a token in fact. She got her wood in good time, but only a disgraceful amount of groveling by the proprietors of the hotel persuaded Curt and Laurence to get a small amount for the hotel. They simply felt that while the widow was unable to do for herself, the proprietors looked husky and could get their own wood. The money in both cases was irrelevant.

The local economic system would have been a good deal easier to understand if there had been no money involved at all. But money did play a role in the valley. There were a number of commercial enterprises in Stehekin: the lunch counter, the hotel, a pack string, Harry's apple orchard and the cream that was sent downlake by the Maxwells and the Courtneys. There were also opportunities for paid employment by the government via the Post Office and the Forest Service. These, however, were regarded as so irrational as to be wholly outside the realm of economics.

Two features, then, were common to most of the money transactions at Stehekin. First, money largely involved outsiders. Second, money was a seasonal matter; it could be acquired, with a few exceptions, only when the snow was gone. These factors were closely related and had a series of implications. One was a two-price system. Certainly such an arrangement is not unknown outside Stehekin, but it is usually associated with monopoly, kickbacks and other dubious characteristics of latter-day capitalism. In Stehekin, however, it was simply a consequence of the uneasy compromise the valley had found itself forced into by the existence of downlake and its cold-cash nexus. Outsiders lived by money and to relate to downlake it was necessary to deal in money. So money had to be got, and the only place money came from was downlake; hence the various businesses and jobs mentioned. Prices and wages either were set by downlakers or were taken from the Sears catalogue or, in the case of food, from advertisements of downlake chain stores. The figures arrived at were obviously satisfactory to outsiders, but they were ridiculous to Stehekinites and could not be charged to friends and neighbors. So, if there was a service—hauling something or other by truck, say—that had a going price to the government or other summer visitors, it was unthinkable that would be the price to a genuine valley resident. The price was either nothing or a fraction of the general market price. The issue was simply a matter of plain decency.

There was also a striking difference in the price of labor by season. We discovered this when Jane bemoaned her lack of kitchen shelves during our first winter. Curt had some pine lumber stashed away and soon Jane was after him to build those shelves. In no time at all she had outlined cabinet work requiring a good bit of skill. Curt agreed to make them and one snowy day showed up with an armload of tools. We had some coffee and talked about life for an hour or two. Then Curt went back home for lunch and was back at two. He cut a couple of boards, had some more coffee, and went home.

He was back a day or so later and cut a few more boards and we learned more about the valley. The process went on all winter and we began to wonder how we could ever calculate what we owed for what eventually turned out to be quite splendid cabinets; but we had, after all, made a blank contract. The day eventually came when the job was finished and we asked Curt what we owed him. He was dumbfounded.

"Why, nothing at all. You don't think I'd charge *neighbors* for this, do you?"

"But, good lord, Curt, you've spent weeks on this and it's a great job. We owe you money."

"No, I couldn't take anything from you. You live up here now. And what's more, this is off season."

"What do you mean?"

"Well, you see, all the cash we get up here comes in the summer. My labor isn't worth anything in the winter. So I couldn't charge you for this anyhow."

We argued vigorously over a period of several days. Finally, Curt saw that we were deeply troubled and agreed to a compromise. A protracted period of bargaining followed before a figure was agreed upon. It was that process of oriental market haggling that economists like to cite as the prototype of the market economy. Save for one thing, that is, and this was that the roles of buyer and seller were exactly reversed: the buyer (us) was pushing the price up and the seller (Curt) was pushing it down. We all felt relieved when the thing was settled.

While we managed to settle this particular issue, the matter of money continued to disturb us—and not simply for its lack. The truth was that we had touched on the fundamental ambiguity of Stehekin. It was not just a simple subsistence economy, it was also a money economy of however small and primitive a sort. Where the two impinged, as with our kitchen cabinets, there was uncertainty and uneasiness. The natural Stehekin system relied on the ideas of need, ability, and neighborliness. But there was also downlake and it relied on money. Had Stehekin been able to draw the mountain walls shut just a little more tightly, things might have been better; certainly they would have been clearer. But people did come up the lake. There were definite things that came from downlake that were essential, and others that were unfortunately merely desirable. Perhaps it could all have been kept in manageable bounds if it had not been for the Sears Roebuck catalogue. I don't know. At any rate we had discovered the virus that was ultimately to change the character of the valley community.

Everyone in the valley struggled with the problem. The most common answers to the dilemma of deciding which set of values to follow at any given point were those that Curt had cited: the difference of seasons and the difference between valley people and downlake people. Skinny Wilson had a different answer. He had been a plumber outside when he received a sudden inheritance and put down his tools and moved to Stehekin while still fairly young. As an exception to the general rule that nobody was highly skilled, he still knew how to plumb a house and do it well. So his solution was to charge current union wages on any plumbing job. And he worked a regular union day on such occasions, beginning precisely at eight and quitting at five. Fortunately, he would ignore other union rules in such ways as letting me work

alongside him on my own home without having an appren-
tice's card. His solution seemed queer in Stehekin, but it was
accepted.

In more direct dealings with downlake such as buying
things, of course, there was no compromise. We had to send
money and that was all there seemed to it. Even here, however, things occasionally took on an air of absurdity. The
most common point of contact with the downlake world was
Sears Roebuck. The Courtneys, for example, would settle
down around the kitchen table sometime after the summer
had ended and the paid jobs had stopped, probably after the
first serious-looking snow had arrived. They would count
their earnings and open the Sears catalogue. Everyone would
have necessities to order before winter really began: mittens,
wool sox, some heavy pants, a new axe and so on. The things
actually ordered were pretty much genuine necessities, but
this, of course, did not preclude long hours of dreaming over
some of the luxuries so luringly pictured.

On these occasions Mamie Courtney, selfless though she
was, used to look longingly at the page with the big pressure
cooker. She regularly put up several hundred quarts of food,
but did it by the old laborious method of steaming on top of
the range for many hours. The pressure cooker would have
cut all this short and, so the catalogue said, be much better. It
was not to be thought of seriously, however; the price was
over twenty dollars. And so, year after year, the big order
went out for only the really mundane things.

One year, however, that wonderfully oiled machine of
Sears Roebuck slipped a gear. Along with the items ordered
for winter there came a huge box. It contained just that pres-

sure cooker Mamie had dreamed of—and it was more beautiful than the picture had intimated. The Courtneys examined it and checked the order slips to make sure nobody had given way to temptation; nobody had. Regretfully, they repacked the cooker and mailed it back with a note that it had not been ordered.

The mail a week later brought a printed communication from Sears expressing regret they had not liked the pressure cooker and enclosed a check for the price at which it was listed. Carefully, the Courtneys wrote back saying this was for a pressure cooker which had come unordered. They enclosed the check. The next week's mail brought back the pressure cooker. This time the Courtneys capitulated.

There are points beyond which irrationality can only be humored.

4.

The process of our acculturation must have been going on throughout that first winter,

but we were hardly aware of it other than that we saw we had a lot to learn. Other changes were taking place in us, though; changes of which we were largely insensible. I suppose that these could be described in large and impressive terms: world outlook, ideology, value system or whatnot. Actually the issues were largely practical and matter of fact: what should be done today and what left for some tomorrow, whether or not to meet the boat, whether to call on some of the neighbors across the river. Many of these were matters of choice and not determined by necessity. It made one more thoughtful perhaps, but certainly different in a way difficult to define from downlake routines. The difference appeared in our sense of attitudes toward what everyone in the valley called, simply, downlake.

Downlake was more of a noun than an adverb. You could say that you were going downlake and outsiders would take it to mean merely travelling in a particular direction, but to a local it meant that you were headed for a definite place—as one might say, "I'm going to Tahiti or Timbuctu." And it usually meant a good deal more than this: I'm heading into a different world and I'm not too happy about it. The plain fact was that the people of downlake were different. They were driven and they were irrational; they lived by rules that had no basis in common sense and seemed to have given up whatever humanity they had been born with. It was the dawning of this sense of deep difference that marked our real acculturation.

It wasn't that downlake was perceived as hostile. It was rather than downlake was impersonal, unpredictable and irrational. What went on there seemed to be largely a matter of chance and accident. This sense of uncertainty inclined one to remain aloof and not to have anything more to do with downlake than could be absolutely helped. This most definitely went for actually going downlake one's self, which was to be avoided if at all possible. We were dependent on downlake in a number of ways, however much we would have liked to deny it. A toothache or appendicitis could send one down, and so could a really catastrophic breakdown of an essential piece of machinery. And there were crises of other sorts, most of which were of equal or greater unpleasantness

—anything that called for seeing a lawyer, say. And the keenness of the distaste for going downlake meant that the going was invariably put off to the last conceivable moment, as when the toothache got really unbearable or the appendix had actually burst.

The ordeal of going began almost immediately, once you had steeled yourself to getting on the boat. With cast off, you were adrift and cut off from everything that gave support. And the trip was definitely downhill. The tourists who asked how much higher the upper end of the lake was were actually correct, at least in a figurative sense. As the boat proceeded, the cliffs and peaks gradually diminished to hills that were more and more rounded and lesser in every way. The forest alongside grew thinner and the land more arid. Houses and other buildings appeared and grew dense upon a space that might have had some charm had it been left untouched. The trip became interminable and the seats hard. Where the trip up was one of mounting excitement and drama approaching Stehekin and looking up to the peaks of McGregor, Buckner and Booker with their shining snows, this was one of letdown and anticlimax. The sense of this was overwhelming even if there happened to be no specific ordeal waiting at the lower end.

Things got worse as soon as you stepped off the boat. There was the hassle of grabbing your baggage in the midst of a scramble of the other passengers getting their own. They were all in a hurry and ordinary politeness had no part in the scene. Perhaps you would find that your bag had been put off at the Twenty-five Mile Creek stop, and you'd have to go through a frantic effort to sort that one out. Once you had your bag, you walked up the dock to the main street of

Chelan. Here there were—well, maybe not actual crowds, but always lots of people. You could stare at someone walking right toward you and he would merely stare straight ahead as though you didn't exist. No greeting at all. Then you would be walking along the road to wherever you were going to spend the night, obviously and conspicuously carrying a bag. Automobiles and trucks would be going your way—and nobody would stop to offer a lift. And worse, anything you wanted or needed would take money. Everyone expected to be paid, whether he actually had his hand out or not. It even seemed that if you wanted somebody just to talk to, you had to pay.

About this time a mix of fury and panic would begin to take over. If there were a boat leaving to go back uplake, you'd probably be on it. But you were stuck, and if the time were other than summer when the boat went every day, you'd have to wait over at least two nights and a day. That was probable in summer too, since anything you had to do—like see the dentist—had to take place during hours that didn't include evening. Nobody cared in the least how much you were hurting.

So you would hole up someplace at a thoroughly ridiculous price and spend the evening sucking on that tooth and thinking about Stehekin. If you were walking along the road back there, you'd know that the first car that came along would stop and give you a ride; or if it were going the opposite way, would give you a chance to chat with the driver. And if there were no cars on the road, you'd know you could walk home since home wasn't that far. If you met somebody else afoot, whether you knew him or not, you'd greet him and pass the time of day. If you were having some kind of problem, you'd know that you could go to the nearest house and get help. Downlake you were just a stranger where that was an ugly word.

The feeling that most Stehekinites had about downlake extended to the few among them who tended to go downlake more than absolutely necessary. Anyone who went downlake under any circumstances was likely to bring back whatever bug was going around in that pestilential world. Since most of us hardly ever went, we had little immunity to the maladies that afflicted those unfortunate people. Thus, when a germ did appear in Stehekin, it would get passed around to lots of us. And there would inevitably be a casting about as to who had been downlake and brought back the disease. By common consent, the disease would be labelled with the name of the guilty individual. It was not exactly a mark of shame, but then it was nothing to be proud about, either.

By any objective standard, the people of Stehekin were hard workers. They put forth large amounts of effort and energy for survival and modest comfort. Yet there was always the implicit charge from downlakers that there was something wrong about it all, that Stehekinites must be lazy or otherwise deficient to be content not to strive for achievement like normal Americans. Everyone felt this from visitors in one way or another. It usually came out in the form of the question: "What do you do in the winter?" There wasn't any use in trying to answer this one, and we, like the neighbors, soon gave up trying. The charitable explanation was that nobody who had not lived through a Stehekin winter quite knew what was involved. But it was irritating all the same.

In all probability, at least some of the visitors who asked that question and others like it knew better than the query implied on its face. With them it was an attack—or maybe a counterattack to what they felt to be contempt for their own life patterns. It was a dialogue of some subtlety—almost always below the surface, and almost impossible to open up for debate across the line between the two worlds.

It would be a mistake to assume that everyone in Stehekin was clear-headed about all this. Just as there was a real area of uncertainty on economic arrangement in the valley, there was a zone of deep uneasiness about other downlake values. So judgments were sometimes passed that were based on the ethic of work and getting ahead. Somebody had not got his wood in before snow came; so and so ought to have fixed his roof, done this or done that. These charges could be related to genuine and objective Stehekin needs, but there was generally the downlaker charge of shiftlessness and lack of ambition as well. True, the charge didn't have much steam in it, but it had to be asserted every so often like a ritual all the same.

At first glance, striving and achieving did seem to have a place in the valley. Probably the biggest striver was O. P. Maxwell, a dour rancher who had the place farthest up the valley, right where McGregor sweeps up seven thousand feet from the valley floor. His land was not the best—it was rocky and dry, and for three months in the winter the sun never reached his cabin. Yet he had worked his tail off and managed to clear a good bit of acreage. To get water onto his fields for the hot dry summers, he dug a ditch from the river upstream from his place down across some of the rockiest terrain imaginable, and did it all by hand. The thing must have been three quarters of a mile long and it took years. From time to time he would hire Curt and Laurence Courtney to work on it since he was all alone. Their pay was just a few cents an hour and he drove them unmercifully during the time they put in. Perhaps the capstone of his success as an employer was the time when, just after he had paid Curt and Laurence off, he sold them a decrepit Model T for the full amount they had collected: fifteen dollars. It was their first time at the helm of a car, and they felt a great thrill as they got it started and headed down the valley. They managed to get a couple of miles before it quit. The bargain might have seemed a bad one except that, right then and there, the two of them settled down to take the contraption apart and learn why it had worked in the first place. You might even say this was the launching of two careers, for they emerged from the experience with not only an operating Ford but a fundamental knowledge of mechanics as well. When Laurence ultimately left the valley it was to become an over-the-road trucker, driving the biggest rigs over the worst western mountain passes. And Curt—well, Curt stayed in the valley to preach and practice the ultimate in rational doctrines, the rationality of machines.

There was something inspiring about Curt's certainty. To him there was never any doubt that a given machine could be got to work, never the slightest hint of mystery in even the most recalcitrant and misbegotten pile of rusted junk that held wheels and cogs. Such things had been put together with intelligence and they had purposes; one—anyone—had only to reason it all out and think logically to restore life and action to them. And in truth he invariably proved his point. It might be with something monstrous, like a cast-off, worn-out truck/cement mixer that he found downlake and had shipped up to the valley. Or it might be a broken Swiss music box that looked lost inside one of his hands. Both emerged from his ministrations working. The methods used were different in these examples: the cement mixer required brutal techniques with heavy tools; the music box merely took a sliver of wire peeled off a bit of window screen. Neither device was a familiar item to Curt at the beginning, but both were machines, and with such things rationality *had* to prevail—and it did.

For Curt, machines were ends in themselves. The fact that they could be looked on as instruments and tools to do work with was simply incidental, although a useful argument to be used with unbelievers. If there was a job that could be done either with the use of a machine or by hand (as for example turning an ice cream freezer), use of the machine was to be preferred (hook up a belt to an old car engine) even though the human effort and time involved might be greater. It was this purity of outlook that distinguished Curt's view from that of technological society downlake. He never accepted the instrumental view of that other culture.

This outlook of Curt's, one shared to a lesser degree by most of the valley, had several sides to it. On the one hand, it involved a horror for the throw-away propensities of downlake. Where the impulse downlake seemed invariably to start with a new machine—or at least to get a new part—when something broke down, in Stehekin such an approach was only the direst of last resorts. True, parts did have to be sent for and sometimes they even had to be bought new, but this was only justifiable in cases where a larger assembly would otherwise have to be hauled to the dump. At the same time, the outlook also meant that nothing was ever really thrown away, as we learned when Jane purloined the oven rack. So it just lay out in the open or off in the bushes which grew up around it when it temporarily became boring.

The other difference was that function tended to follow machinery rather than vice versa. You had the machine and looked for uses for it instead of looking for a machine to do some job. We became quite conscious of this in the one area where collectively we were considered to have useful knowledge—that is, in Jane's training on matters relating to health. It came about when Art Peterson was trying to get his sawmill set up. The job involved an apparently endless use of an emery grinder. There was a pair of protective goggles hanging by the grinder; but nobody seemed ever to bother with it since there was a continuing procession of men coming up to Jane asking her to get bits of metal out of their eyes. With a number of these injuries, Jane was successful in removing the bits with a light touch of a sterile cotton swab. With others, however, quite a number in fact, the objects were so imbedded that she felt compelled to desist and administer instructions (as taught by the Yale School of Nursing) to go see a doctor—even though this involved going downlake—and to be more careful in the future.

After several such cases, Jane became aware that her instructions were not being followed, and that recoveries had nonetheless occurred. At first she dared to hope that she had wrought better than she knew. But that wasn't the truth. She cornered one of these cases and demanded to know what had happened. The fellow shuffled his feet, cleared his throat and tried to escape. Finding he couldn't, he confessed that everyone with a piece of metal in his eye went to Curt—after having been directed futilely by Curt to Jane. Well, what had Curt done? You see (this said with the acutest of embarrassment), Curt had taken the sliver out with a magnet.

It was humiliating. And Curt knew it as well as she did and had tried to prevent her learning about his role. Moreover, he had done his best to protect her jurisdiction by sending patients to her first, even though he knew she probably wasn't much good at the task. When she talked to Curt about it, he was apologetic; and to make up for what he had done to her ego, he presented her with his bit of surgical magic. It was an ugly black tar-covered object about five inches long with a couple of wires sticking out of each end. What was it? Well, sir, that was the coil from an old Model T, and Curt had had it kicking around for a long time out in the shop. You just took a couple of batteries like those in the telephone and hooked them up to one end and . . . he showed her just how. Jane did her best to be gracious about it and accepted the gift. But it wasn't the sort of thing that Yale School of Nursing really approved.

So old O. P. Maxwell did make his mark—on Curt and Laurence, if not much of any other way. His ranch got bigger clearings and there was water on part of it. But as a farm it really didn't amount to much. It was nine miles from his place to the dock and the snow was heavy up his way. He had a few cows that he kept in a little log barn through the winter, and he marketed the cream. Each boat day he would strap a five-gallon can of cream on his back and snowshoe it down to the dock. It was a rough life and he worked hard at it.

He was really pretty unsociable, and the other people in the valley tended to leave him alone, even to mistrust him a bit. Still, even he had to cooperate at times, as when it was time to get a bull up into the valley. Then there would be dickering and haggling with the Courtneys and maybe Harry

Buckner over who would get a bull to be shared, or whether they should get together and bring one in temporarily. There was a good deal of tension about this. Curt and Laurence didn't forget about the way he had worked them on the ditch.

And they didn't forget how mad and ungrateful he had got when he had them clear the snow off his shed roof. The shed had a pretty steep roof, but it tended to catch a big load of heavy snow. The structure wasn't too well braced, so most years it had to be freed from the load. Neither Curt nor Laurence really liked to shovel snow, so they had worked out a fine technique for doing the job. They would take a length of Forest Service telephone wire and get up on the peak of the roof. They would trample the wire down to the shakes and then, with one at each end of the shed, they would pull and sort of saw the wire down one side of the roof. As the wire reached the eave, the whole load of snow on that side would slide off. It was very soul-satisfying when it worked right.

One time, however, there was an awful lot of snow and it was heavy. Getting the wire down to the eave took a lot of sawing, but finally it broke through. Then the snow slid. But this time, that wasn't all. The snow on the opposite side stayed in place and the building began to quiver. And then it began to creak and crack—as Curt put it, the thing shook like a dog coming out of water. And then the whole thing came crashing down in the direction on which the snow had been cleared. After that, they just gave up trying to get along with O. P. Maxwell.

Just why Maxwell drove himself as hard as he did is hard to say. He didn't have any immediate family and ultimately his place went to a couple of his brothers, who came in and operated the place for a number of years without trying to keep the irrigation ditch open or clearing more land, as he had done. Maybe he had a puritan upbringing, but that theory leaves a puzzle still, since his two brothers showed no trace of anything like that. Probably the explanation was a lot simpler: he just hated to go downlake.

I suppose it would be easy to take O. P. Maxwell as the true Stehekinite, the archetype. He was solitary, unsociable and not very communicative (except when he had something like that shed to talk about). But that wasn't so. Some of the others were sociable, most were talkative—in fact, there wasn't anybody who could top Hugh for story telling. The problem was to get him to bring it to an end. And Harry loved the dock—he seldom missed a boat day; even Sundays, when there wasn't any sensible reason for going down to the lake. The weather could be awful and the road an ordeal. It might cost him the best part of the day, but he would get to the dock, either by carbucking the snow or using the team and the sled when a car couldn't make it. So there he always was when the boat came in. There would generally be somebody on the boat Harry knew, just from having been on hand when he had come in before. He would remember Harry and Harry would remember him, or act as though he did.

So if Maxwell was the big striver, Harry was something else. And oddly enough, you'd have to call him the valley's achiever. He had the one real commercial farm in the valley, apples, acres and acres of apple trees. He had come into the valley to help his uncle, Henry Buckner—the one whose name is tacked on to Buckner Mountain, the peak with the two glaciers you see as you look up the valley from Stehekin

—and they had cleared land with a team of horses and a stump puller. That's hard work, really hard work; but they managed to get a big clearing that they put into orchard, and there was a fine view across to Rainbow Falls, which you could hear from the house at the opposite edge of the orchard. And there was McGregor standing up at the far end of the ridge, sharp-pointed and for most of the year white-faced to the ragged edges of its cliffs.

Harry and his uncle built a barn and later Harry built a big packing shed with a cement floor that was great for square dancing, and Harry learned to be a fine caller for the dances. The house had a fireplace Harry had built and there was a spot outdoors with a table and a fireplace with chairs and all, and you could sit out there in the evening swapping stories with Harry and the others and watching the light on McGregor and listening to the falls in the background and it was just about the finest spot you had ever been in. Everybody liked it and everybody turned up there, people from the valley and downlakers as well, always a crowd.

Harry was the one man in the valley the downlakers couldn't cut. He was doing something useful—growing apples, like they were. Sure, they would go out into his orchard and make remarks about this or that, but you could see that this was simple envy for what Harry had managed for himself and his family. And he got some cash income out of the orchard. That made him a good man, even if the money wasn't all that big by downlake standards. The thing was that he had to pay those big freight charges on the barge to get his apples to market. This hurt, but he had an advantage the downlakers had lost long ago. The orchardists at the other end of the lake had long been obliged to spray their trees with a big array of poisons; one kind for this bug, another for that, and then still another and another. This of course took a lot of money, and since these bugs had not yet found their way up-lake, Harry could still sell his apples and ship them out at a modest profit. His apples were better because they were not loaded with all those poisons, but in the marketing they were mixed up with the others, so he never got the extra price he should have. However, he did have the satisfaction of providing apples to several downlake orchardists for their own use; they knew what was good, as well as safe.

So Harry had the best of both worlds. He had a handsome place; things were maybe cobbled up in a lot of places, but even the unpainted boards on his house had taken on a deep rich color from the weather and it was really fine looking. And he had a fine family with his wife and three daughters. So he was a man of substance, dealing with the downlake marketers and doing something serious, raising apples. Only really he was just letting the trees grow the apples and he spent a lot of his time fishing in the river where it bordered his place and going to the dock. Of course, most of the people from downlake who came to his place didn't know all this; they just thought he was a sound man.

Maybe there's some law of nature that says such things can't go on. Whether or not this is true, there were some lesser laws of nature that brought it to an end. First of all, the girls grew up. All three of them were handsome and they all got married and left the valley. They had been the backbone of Harry's labor force during those times when the orchard did take a lot of work, thinning, picking and sorting. The next thing was that the bugs at last found the valley. I don't mean that Stehekin didn't have bugs of its own—it did, lots of them. But these were things like mosquitoes, yellowjackets and blackflies that can make humans miserable. What was new was the sort of bugs that specialize in apples programmed for New York. So it was up to Harry to begin spraying the orchard. It was just for the one kind of bug, I suppose, but Harry knew that this would be just the beginning. So he didn't spray. There was a small crop or two that could be sent downlake after that, but the trees were old now and Harry stopped pruning and the apples just fell to the ground. Anyone was welcome to come and help himself. People had always done that, but it wasn't the same. There wasn't a party in the packing shed for making cider and so on and, in fact, the packing shed collapsed one winter. So, when Beryl quit as postmaster, Harry took the job; and then he really had to go to the dock every day.

Achieving, then, just wasn't what the valley was all about. This was obvious enough, but it was surprising how many people drew the wrong conclusions. There was a small, steady stream of individuals who came into the valley and announced they were going to stay forever. Mostly they were strays of some kind. That was all right, of course; everyone in the valley had some kind of feeling, as I said, about things downlake, so there was a certain amount of sympathy for those who came uplake just wanting to escape from something or other. For some of them it was just what they needed—a chance to lick their wounds, see a little friendliness and then move on again. Like the girl who had been abandoned with a couple of kids: the valley really mobilized for her. Then one day she took off to see about some other kids she had and hadn't mentioned, leaving the one batch with the Bells. She stayed away and stayed away and the Bells got to wondering. But finally she came back, took the kids and went downlake. And there was one old fellow that showed up from nowhere along in the fall and set up camp near Rainbow Falls. He put his stuff in the privy and somebody thought he even slept there. The valley got worried about him, took him food and blankets the tried to get him in under cover somewhere, but he wouldn't allow that. Finally word came that he had escaped from a state mental hospital on the west side and had come over the pass; that was why nobody had seen him arrive. They came and got him.

The only one of these strays who really stayed was Andy. He didn't have a grudge against the world like a lot of the others, but he did have, as the saying goes, a problem with alcohol, that and maybe a case of tuberculosis he didn't talk about. The alcohol problem gave him just enough of an incentive that you might say he became an achiever in a small way. He managed to fix up a little shack on a piece of land whose owner either didn't care or didn't know about it, and he got hold of an old bus that had been brought up for taking people up the road. He got it to running and would meet the boat during the summer and take people to see Rainbow Falls before the boat went back. And every now and then there would be a crowd that wanted to go clear to the end of the road, and Andy was game for that. If there was a late start through trouble with the bus or something, he would go anyhow. And when it got dark where he really needed to see to drive—like along the bluff above Tumwater where the river goes through a narrow gorge just below—he would stop and get out an old beat-up gasoline lantern, light it and hang it on the radiator cap, take a slug of whisky and go on. He never lost a passenger and I'd hate to say he didn't live a good life to the end.

But some of the others really had it all wrong. There were a number who figured all there was to life in Stehekin was hunting and fishing. They thought they could live on those two items and didn't even see any reason to speak to anybody. They all found that there were a few difficulties. First, the various things that Stehekinites did and that looked so simple weren't so easy after all. And second, these fellows all turned out to be poor fishermen and worse hunters. Anyhow, even if they had been really good at these things they would still have gone hungry. Then there was the family that came because the wife was a compulsive spendthrift. Their idea was that since Stehekin had no stores, it would hold economic salvation. But they forgot about Sears Roebuck, so they gave up after a while.

And so the procession went. They would come in, some with a lot of stuff shipped up on the barge and others with not much of anything. Maybe they would manage to get a start on building some kind of cabin, or maybe they would stay in some shack that was vacant or abandoned. Then after a time—it might even be a few years—the signs would develop: they would start going downlake for one reason or other and you'd know it wouldn't be long. Then, without their saying much to anybody, they would leave and you'd never see them again. The funny thing was that in the end they were just like the really short-term visitors: they never saw the valley or its country, and they never knew it.

On the one hand, then, the essential characteristic of Stehekin as a community was that it was not commercial. Commercial activities did take place, especially during the summer and on a small scale, but nobody's heart was in any of them. On the other hand, the true test of a Stehekinite was that reluctance to go downlake.

Stehekinites met this test with varying degrees of fervor. Probably the winner of a contest for purity of outlook on this score would have been O. P. Maxwell. He hardly ever went down and when he did, it was for something really dire. At any rate, it was pretty dire when he went down for the last time. The neighbors had been noticing that there was a lump in the middle of his forehead and it was getting bigger. This went on for a while before anyone got up the nerve to say anything to him about it. Finally, however, several people went to him when he was at the dock one day in early spring. They told him he ought to go downlake and see a doctor. He sort of growled at them that he didn't want to go downlake and he didn't trust doctors. But they kept after him, and finally he agreed to go.

He went down one Wednesday and was back on Friday. He didn't say anything to anybody and nobody felt like asking him what he had learned. But someone knew the doctor and found out what had happened. He had seen the doctor on Thursday and the doctor had taken a biopsy and then had told him he had to go into the hospital and have the lump taken off. So Maxwell replied,

"Well, all right, if you can do it right away."

"Oh, we can't do that. We have to arrange for the operating room and so on. It will take a few days. And then you'll have to stay in the hospital."

"But I have to get back uplake to milk and feed the cows. Have to go back on the Friday boat."

"You just can't go. If you don't have this done now you'll be dead in six months."

"Well," he replied, "I still have to take care of the cows. Goodbye."

And he came back uplake on Friday. And he didn't go back down. But he seemed to be all right. In fact, the lump got to looking smaller. And finally it just disappeared. Everyone was pretty curious about it but nobody wanted to say anything to him about it. Finally, though, somebody got nerve up and asked him about the lump he used to have.

"You know that dehorning medicine I got for the cows? Well, I. . . . "

He lived for several more years.

5.

Even after I had come
to understand
the true importance of the mail
in Stehekin, it was still a mystery why other
forms of communication should have played so
large a part in the life of the valley. On the face of
things there wasn't very much to communicate,
and doing it was the cause for an endless amount
of trouble.

The telephone was the outstanding case.
There had been a telephone line in the valley for
almost as long as anyone could remember. It had
been built by the Forest Service when that
agency was active in the area. Its purpose was to

deal with forest fires. The line, a naked but heavy gauge wire of superlative material—superlative, that is, for wiring spreading woodshed rafters back into place and a multitude of other essential Stehekin uses—ran from the guard station near the dock sixteen miles up the valley to Bridge Creek, with various spurs to lookout points on McGregor, and for a while to Goode Ridge and a couple of other subsidiary stations. These points were manned during the worst fire seasons so they could report strikes of lightning and any resulting fires. But, either as an addition to the number of reporting stations or as a concession to the valley residents, a number of the older households were hooked in to the line.

Fastened to the wall at each station was an ungainly looking instrument consisting of a large box with a protruding mouthpiece, an earpiece hanging from a hook, a pair of bells atop and a crank at the side. To make a call, you consulted a handwritten placard beside the instrument, lifted the earpiece, and twirled the crank appropriately. Somebody would answer—probably the person you had called, if the batteries in his instrument weren't too weak. But whether you got the right person or not, you always got Mrs. Lesh.

Mrs. Lesh was one of the few people in the valley who never went by her first name. In fact, nobody seemed to know it; and for all I could tell, Missus was her name. At any rate, she was a small and seemingly fragile woman who seldom went out of her house. Her fragility, however, was largely illusion; as she repeatedly betrayed herself when there was some crisis that had to be dealt with. Her appearance, nonetheless, must have been highly useful to her, as when the bear got to messing around her place while Frank was downlake.

The Leshes lived apart from the rest of the valley and most of us saw rather little of them, which was apparently the way they liked it. And yet, they were always cordial when we dropped by for their outgoing mail; and Mrs. Lesh fairly lived by the telephone. In one sense they were genuine old-timers. Frank had been in the valley many years before and had attempted to run one of the first of a series of little saw-mills which had been in the valley. Then they moved out and didn't reappear until a bit before the war. Frank got Jack Blankenship to build him a good-sized log house and they settled in it. There was some kind of mystery about them—just what I never knew; for Stehekin, despite its love of gossip, had retained that frontier quality of respect for anybody's reticence about his past. Reputedly there was somebody in the valley who had come to it as a hideout from the law—the usual story was that the offense was selling liquor to the Indians, but that seemed rather archaic. At any rate it wasn't Frank, who once revealed his outside occupation was dynamiting oil well fires. But he didn't talk much; that he left to his wife and the telephone.

Sometime after they moved in, Frank hooked himself up to the Forest Service line. He didn't bother about getting authorization; he just tied in with what he had handy, which was barbed wire. It made a frightful racket over the entire system. In fact, it really *sounded* like barbed wire. And the line sagged low in a lot of places, particularly over the road, where it almost decapitated a youngster riding in the back of somebody's truck one day. That precipitated action, and the Forest Service tried to disconnect Frank. He wouldn't have that, so he found some abandoned phone line from one of the old lookouts and strung it up to the house.

So each time the phone rang, whether it was the extraordinary five shorts that meant there was a fire or some emergency and everybody was to get on the line, or some other ring, Mrs. Lesh was right there. Considering that this system was a survival from the original telephone systems throughout the United States, it seems amazing that the idea should ever have grown up that a telephone conversation is private. Bugging was built in from the start.

With the barbed wire gone, however, the line worked reasonably well. At any rate, anyone who had an instrument was treated to recurrent jingles of longs and shorts. Since longs and shorts tended to be undistinguishable, most people waited for a couple of repeats of anything that might have been calls for them and let the person at the crank get a little crisper in his or her rings. It made for a lot of noise and we were glad not to be connected. But we had reason to hate the system all the same.

Unfortunately, there was a second phone line. It went downlake, hanging from stanchions driven into the rocky cliffs along the western side. Its one merit was that avalanches wiped it out every winter and then it caused no trouble. At best it never worked very well, but there were times when conditions were good and one could go down to Daisy Weaver's at the head of the lake (you had to row a mile to get to her place) and could actually talk to Chelan. The evil of this line was simply that it existed. Theoretically, the downlake line could be switched onto the valley line so that somebody at our end of the valley could talk with Chelan. Much worse, the downlake line could be switched into the general phone system and we could talk to San Francisco, Chicago, New York, or Moscow. This was, of course, nonsense; nobody in Stehekin wanted to talk to San Francisco, Chicago, New York, or Moscow, and this included us.

In actuality, it was impossible. The human voice was so hideously distorted by those wires and switches that nothing meaningful could be got beyond Chelan even if it ever reached that point. This was vaguely known in Stehekin, although few people had direct experience of it. It was most definitely not known elsewhere. Downlake, even as far back as World War II, was convinced there was no place unreachable by telephone, and to argue otherwise was to invite utter discredit.

My own appreciation of this began one stormy night when we had been long in bed. There was a pounding at the door and I struggled up to find Hugh. He was thoroughly drenched and had obviously walked the nearly half mile from his place.

"There's a long distance call for you, " he said as he shook off his hat.

"What? I mean, who's it from? Uh—how do you know?"

"Don't know who it's from. Beryl phoned up from the head of the lake. She says the Chelan operator has been trying to get through for hours, now. Had a lot of difficulty hearing Chelan."

He looked at me impatiently while I tried to wake up and take in the magnitude of the occasion.

"I don't know anybody in Chelan who'd call me," I said finally.

"But it's not from Chelan. That's what I'm trying to tell you."

"Where?"

"Beryl can't make out—California or New York maybe."

I pondered. There wasn't anybody in California or New York who really needed to talk with me about anything in a rush, and I couldn't think of anything I wanted to say, either. I was on the point of telling this to Hugh when I looked at him. He was still dripping from his walk and was obviously getting exasperated with my shilly-shallying.

"The road's pretty bad with all this water, but Laurence will run you down. He's warming up the truck. Get your pants on."

I was about to protest, but it was obvious that to Stehekin, a long distance call had to be a life-and-death matter; it was also apparent that the valley was well on its way to a major mobilization to meet my crisis. Since there was nothing I could do either to stop the mobilization or to interpret outside telephone habits to Hugh, I dressed and walked down to Courtneys with him and hopped in the truck beside Laurence.

At the dock, lights were on at Blankenship's and Jack had a fire going and Beryl was making coffee. She had talked several times to Chelan.

"It's kind of hard to hear the girl in Chelan, but I'll try to get through," she said.

I listened for a moment and then leaned against the wall, picked up the receiver and put my mouth to the instrument. There was a fearful clatter of screeches and buzzings in my ear. However, from time to time there was a sound faintly reminiscent of the human voice. It came and went. I yelled my name and my questions. More screeches. Finally Beryl and then Jack tried. The only thing they got from it was that there was a long-distance call for me, and that Chelan was willing to relay. Only none of us could make out Chelan. After what seemed like hours, everybody gave up, emotionally and physically exhausted.

What happened, of course, was that several weeks later a letter came from an acquaintance of mine in the Midwest who casually mentioned having tried to get me by phone to see how I was getting on in the hills. When the neighbors asked me concernedly about the meaning of that missed long distance call of mine, I had to make up a story about terrible illness to a beloved relative who had happily recovered.

After that, we warned our friends about the telephone. Or rather, we simply told them there was no telephone in Stehekin (there was no point in going into the real situation). A number of these friends then resorted to telegram. Since their messages usually announced their impending arrival as guests, we had the frequent situation of meeting them in surprise at the dock (if we were at the dock) and then picking up our mail, which contained their telegram. The wire went in to Chelan Falls, where it was mailed, carried to Chelan, sorted and put on the boat for Stehekin. Ordinarily mail was straightforward enough, but there were times when I received a note from the postmaster (one subsequent to Beryl) telling me to come down for a special delivery; all those stamps made the envelope look too important to be entrusted to just anyone who might be coming up the valley.

With all this difficulty with telephones and mails, I suppose someone will suggest that we should have used smoke signals. Oddly enough, there was at least one occasion when this was tried. And in a certain sense, it was successful.

A few years after the war, the Game Commission built themselves a little log cabin in the lower part of the valley. The Game Commission was a long way from being popular in Stehekin, and it had been that way since the 1920's, when, by vivid local account, their people had moved into the valley and trapped the spawn from the then-abundant big cutthroat trout in the river. They shipped this spawn to other parts of the state until it got scarce. Then they moved out, giving their old shack to the valley for a community center. At any rate, there's a sign on the building saying "Community Center," but it hardly got used since its presence still made the local people mad. Anyhow, there wasn't much in the way of formal organization in Stehekin to take care of it. And when the Game Commission wanted a spot for their people to camp and fish and do whatever they thought they were supposed to do, they built a new cabin.

Their hunting and fishing was all right, but when they did things like spreading a lot of high-powered poison around the valley in hunks of meat, it was pretty bad. The idea was that the poison would get the coyotes and there would be more deer for the hunters to kill. This idea was thoroughly discredited long before the Game people came up with their poison, but this didn't stop them any more than protests from the valley did. They managed to kill a good many of the local dogs and maybe some coyotes, too.

The coyote is not a native of these mountains. Coyotes have been hunted and persecuted unmercifully on the plains, and yet they have somehow survived. Some have taken refuge in higher country and have adapted splendidly to the hills. In spite of the way the indigenous predators have been decimated by bounty hunting, coyotes have helped fill an ecological gap, keeping the deer herds thinned out and healthy by picking off the sick and weakling deer, the only ones they can catch.

We used to feel, too, that the coyotes were a fine feature of the valley just for themselves. There were nights when we'd hear them sing. One fellow in particular would sit on the big granite rock at the base of the mountain behind the house and give a concert of fine beauty. He was an exquisite soprano with an utter clarity of tone. He would sing for perhaps a half hour while we lay in bed listening, and at the end of the performance his voice would rise with a perfect *glissando* to a bell-like note right near the upper end of my ability to hear, which he would repeat three times. I don't think it meant anything; it was, very simply, music.

The coyotes were useful as well. They would clean up the carcasses that had been left to rot on the ground by hunters too incompetent to shoot straight and too lazy to pursue the deer they had wounded, a pretty common thing. But the real point is that the coyotes were an end in themselves and should have been so viewed. And once they were seen this way, they were a joy. There have been moments when I have been off from the house—or even sitting by the kitchen window—and suddenly had the sense I was not alone. Maybe something would have caught the corner of my eye. I'd happen to glance to the side, and there would be a coyote sitting on a rock just watching me. I suppose he had been doing this for some time without my being aware of it and was amused by my lack of alertness. After a minute he would move off at a trot and probably be back in another spot a few minutes later. There was companionship in it, and a very good feeling it was.

If the Game Commission was unpopular for their attitude toward the coyotes, they didn't gain much by their approach to Frank Lesh's beaver problem. The beaver had moved into his one-time millpond and were turning his lower acreage into a swamp. He called in the Game people. They came in and trapped out a number of animals, then asked Ray to do the trapping. Ray got quite a number of them and took the pelts to the fur market in Seattle as he was authorized to do. After he came back with the proceeds of his sale—a substantial amount—he quit. As he put it, he liked the beaver a lot better than the people he was selling them to.

The main and continuing source of irritation with the Game Commission, however, was their attitude toward what they called "poaching." The Commission set a hunting season that presumably was based on a nice calculation of the supply of animals. This was a fiction, however, since they made no local studies that might have given them this sort of knowledge. The season was simply set to meet the demands of urban hunters, at a time when it was comfortable to go out in the hills and the animals were in good condition. This was when all the male deer were high on the ridges, however, and could only be got at with elaborate camp outfits and horses. The local people could not take off just then; there were all the things that had to be done to get ready for winter. Moreover, getting the meat down was a problem then. It was far more sensible to wait until the high snows brought the deer down into the valley on their annual migration and it was cool. Then people who needed the meat could get it without taking too much time off and care for it properly. But the Commission's idea was that the deer existed simply for human use, and that use was fun for the "sportsmen." Valley people had to be very circumspect when they adjusted the regulations and reopened the season at a more sensible time. Nobody liked this very much.

There were other absurdities, too. There was a rule, for example, that while you could legally kill a bear that was damaging your property, you couldn't use the hide or the meat. You were supposed to notify the nearest warden, who was supposed to come and get it. But the warden was a long way off and never came up when notified. So there was the prospect of considerable waste. A big bear has a lot of meat, and it can be good.

One fall, one of the neighbors found a bear raising a lot of havoc in some apple trees he had so he shot the bear. The meat was in good condition and he couldn't bear to bury it. He cut it up and shared it with the neighbors. Ray got some of it, and was working outside his cabin one day when a stranger walked up the road and began chatting. Ray, being eminently courteous, invited the fellow in. The man asked a few questions about the valley and then asked if he could have a bit of the roast he saw on the table. Ray served him some and then the fellow asked what kind of meat it was. Ray told him it was bear. At that the man pulled a warden's badge and arrested Ray. Ray refused to say that he had not shot the bear, so he had to go to court, pay a fine and lose his gun. Fortunately there were a few decent people downlake, and they bought the gun at the auction and sent it back to Ray. But it didn't make the "sportsmen's" part of government very well loved in Stehekin.

Stehekinites always had a project hanging in the air to deal with the situation. The plan was that when somebody at the dock saw the Game Commission boat come in—it always had a sneaky, stealthy air—he would get on the phone and give a code message up the valley for people to take appropriate precautions. It may have worked a few times, but in the main, Stehekin was too unorganized to agree on any code word. Still, it would have made a good use for the telephone, at least for the valley line. But the existence of the new Game Commission cabin spoiled the idea. Their people could be camped there and nobody could be sure what they were up to. Mostly we didn't know when they were there, which wasn't very often, after all.

They weren't there at the time of the smoke signal. Elly and Tom (I'm going to name them that in the interest of national security) didn't know this, however. It was a couple of weeks after hunting season and nobody in the valley had so much as seen a deer. But it had turned cool and there was snow up on the ridges and a bone-chilling drizzle was coming down. Elly and Tom decided the conditions were just right to get their deer. So they drove up the valley and parked their car not far from the unoccupied Game Commission cabin and struck off up to the benches above, a fine hunting place when the deer are on their way down. Somewhat later, Lloyd Bell came walking up the valley. As he passed their car, which he recognized, he heard a shot up on the benches nearby. Making a shrewd guess about what had happened, he built a bonfire in front of the empty Game Commission cabin. Just to make sure of things, he piled on some green limbs so there was a lot of smoke. His guess was right: hours later, after dark, Tom and Elly came creeping out of the woods to their car by the cabin, dragging their deer. It must have taken them a couple hours to dry out and warm up. And they never head the last of it.

The telephone was really useful when Mrs. Lesh had to phone about the bear, though. There were always bears around the valley. They had a big area to move around in, and if they got scarce in the American Cascades, there was all of Canada adjoining for more to come from. With just a few exceptions, however, they were black bears (whether they are colored black, brown, or cinnamon); there were almost no grizzlies. This was probably fortunate, since everyone had adjusted to having bears around. For the most part, the local bears were harmless. They lived on berries, carrion, small rodents, grubs, and fresh shoots. Food of this sort kept them busy, and unless they found a garbage dump, they didn't have much concern about humans. So it was normal that when you saw a bear, he'd manage to run before you did.

Garbage, however, is a corrupting thing. Once they find it, bears are apt to stick around. This happened down by the hotel one year when one of the succession of operators decided a bear that started coming around to eat out of the kitchen garbage can was a possible tourist attraction, and actually provided a steady supply of extra rations for him. Within a week, the bear, which had hitherto been a peaceable, normal, wild bear, turned into a mean, demanding and wholly dangerous garbage bear. He had to be shot and we found it hard to forgive that hotel proprietor.

Wild animals in general are rational and peaceful by nature. If they are undisturbed, or simply watched with about the same degree of curiosity which they themselves exhibit, they return the respect they are given. Only a few rules need be followed: don't mess around with any mother with young —bear, deer or any other; don't put them in a corner or seem to threaten them; and don't turn a wild animal into something else. In actuality, only one person has ever been injured by a wild animal in Stehekin. That was Wade Maxwell. He was out behind his place with his dog when the dog took off after a mother bear with a pair of cubs who were quietly digging grubs. The mother bear took after the dog, who ran back to Wade. The bear got close to Wade before she saw him and then laid into him. The dog came to Wade's rescue. He was hurt, but not badly. Nobody could really blame the bear.

But the bear at Leshes was something different. He first appeared in the valley up our way. He made a specialty of breaking into houses that were temporarily vacant, something no ordinary bear would ever do. And he was mean. He went into Ray and Esther's house while they were downlake, going in one window and out another. Ray and Esther came back but left again for an hour, and he came back. Each time, he did purely wanton damage. Twice he threw Esther's knitting basket out in the rain.

We began to suspect we had a real outsider on our hands when he went to O'Neill's place and made a mess. It was vacant, but the O'Neills had tacked a box up on the side of their woodshed and had stacked some cans of motor oil and paint in it. The bear tore it down and bit into every single one of the cans. This was what gave that bear an identity. Each can had a single punch in it from one big canine tooth. It was an old bear and he had lost the other canine. After he had opened all those cans, it was obvious what he had done. Dripping paint and motor oil—he must have had it all over his front—he had gone around the O'Neill's cabin trying to find something he could pull loose. And he couldn't have been in a very good mood from the flavor of paint and oil. There was an almost continuous line around the house.

Then it was our turn. We were away and only found the evidence much later. He had pushed in a window and climbed into the kitchen. Somehow he knew that we had a bin of sugar and another of flour. Both, however, were under the counter. His approach to the problem was direct; he went down through the kitchen counter, that marvel of Curt's carpentry. The results were indescribable. He had emptied the cupboards of our canned goods, and pots and pans were scattered through the woods for a hundred yards. They hadn't done him any good or any harm, but he tossed them around anyhow. I was disgusted enough to take pleasure in one find, though. This was a baseball-shaped mess of metal that had once been a two-pound can of Crisco; he must have had a mighty sore mouth. Maybe that's what made him so angry with us.

Then one night Mrs. Lesh phoned Ray. The bear was sniffing around her house. She had gone out and shooed him away with a broom, but he was back and she didn't like it. So Ray took his Krag and went down to Leshes. He sat up with Mrs. Lesh, waiting for the bear to return. And he did, sniffling around the house. Ray got a window open and Mrs. Lesh stood on tiptoes behind Ray's shoulder. She turned on a flashlight to light up the front sight of the Krag, and Ray shot the bear.

When Ray came to skin the carcass, he understood why the beast had given us so much trouble. There was a lot of buckshot under his hide. It was unquestionably the bear that had raised so much cain, since, indeed, he only had one canine tooth. He was big and he was old. The buckshot was the giveaway, though. He was a bear from outside for sure: no Stehekinite would use buckshot on a bear. And as we thought about his weakness for tin cans, we deduced he was pretty familiar with people and had probably been in trouble elsewhere. So he was almost certainly from someplace out-side the mountains—a city bear, in fact, from Omak, maybe.

Our local bears weren't like that. In fact almost none of the native animals were mean. There were the goats, for example. You would see them in winter along the shores of the lake where the cliffs strike down into the water. They'd be there by the dozen along in February, and they weren't in the least timid. Nothing, except maybe an eagle, could get at them and they knew it. A neighbor once watched a poor scrawny coyote trying hungrily to get at one of the kids cropping the tufts of growth in the cracks of the rocks. The kid was with his mother, who kept a decidedly casual eye on the coyote. The coyote would creep along a ledge toward the kid and the nanny. At the very last moment, the nanny would glance up, nudge the kid, and the two would leisurely hop across a deep crack, leaving the coyote looking foolishly for a way around the crack. I'm sure he never won.

In summer, the goats were miles up above the lake and you'd have to climb up high to see them. There were places where you'd see bits of their wool caught on the brush and you'd actually smell them, but you'd never see them. At other times you'd be out on the face of one of the cliffs hanging five or six thousand feet above the valley, and there they would be, casually walking stiff-legged down a face with an angle of fifty or sixty degrees. They were completely harmless and their meat wasn't much good to eat, but the Game Commission decided to put a regular hunting season on them. Nobody knew how many of them there were, and no attempt was made to find out whether they were increasing or decreasing in number. But the hunt was set all the same.

Perhaps meanness could be claimed for any predator, but

it's hard to view it that way. Predators don't have all that easy a time. Take the marten, for example. The marten belongs to the weasel family, only he is a lot bigger than the ordinary weasel, and will get to be two or two and a half feet long. He has short legs and an elongated appearance, rather like a dachshund. But there's nothing dachshund-like in him otherwise. He's slim and quick and alert. His ears stand up and his eyes are bright as fire. His misfortune is to have about the most gorgeous fur to be found, so he gets hunted and trapped unmercifully. It's a shame, really, for his life is pretty hard.

I saw this one June when I was camped at Pass Creek up the Agnes. The camping spot was small and it lay right between the creek and the trail. I had wakened early and built a fire for coffee perhaps two feet from the trail. While I was warming my hands and urging the coffee on, a snowshoe rabbit came running up the trail about as fast as a rabbit can. All at once he saw me and the fire and stopped dead a matter of inches away. Then he turned and ran back the way he had come. In a few instants he came running back, but this time he utterly ignored me. Behind him by just a matter of seconds came a marten. He was going all out, his belly folding up with each leap so that it must have rubbed against itself. It was a fine show of speed and energy; but although I never heard how the race came out, I will bet on the rabbit.

It was probably much the same with other predators, whether they were mink, fisher, weasel, bobcat or lynx; they all had to work hard for their living. Even the wolverine whose tracks Hugh saw never tried to take advantage of us. But there was one species for which I conceived a deep and pervading personal animosity.

It had to do with our garden. If Jane and I were to continue in Stehekin, we had to do something about our food supply. A garden was obviously part of the answer. So we both set to work, clearing a piece of land, fencing and digging and otherwise fixing up the soil. An awful lot of sweat and tears went into that garden, but the astonishing thing was that things grew for us. It was a miracle, and beautiful to see. There were radishes in no time, leaf lettuce came along nicely, and there were tops of beets and carrots and so on. But the real excitement was the peas. We had been without almost all fresh things through the winter, and any would taste good; but most of all we thought about peas. So we were overjoyed when our garden had peas, large fine strings of them with luxuriant foliage and fine blossoms. Then the petals dropped away and pods began to form. These shaped up nicely, and I broke one or two open. There were peas in them all right, and wonderfully sweet, but still too small. We thought and talked about the next week's harvest.

Then I noticed the pods were disappearing. Mystified, I leaned over the fence and stared at the patch. After a while I knew the worst. A ground squirrel crept out of a hole and started up one of the strings of peas. He took a pod and ate it and then went after another. I threw a rock at him and he ran into his hole. But there were other ground squirrels and we were distraught. We had always thought the ground squirrels rather pleasant. They look like chipmunks except that they have two stripes instead of three and are bigger and not so quick. But they were quick enough. I caught a couple by trap and laid out the carcasses as a warning. It didn't make any difference. There were lots more ground squirrels, and I didn't get any more when I tried poison; I simply taught them to stick to the peas. So I began shooting them with a twenty-two rifle. I became a deadeye shot, but to be the scourge of ground squirrels that I wanted to be, I would have had to be on the job twenty-four hours. In the end, just before the disaster was total, we borrowed a neighbor's house cat, who stopped the mischief promptly. But the ignominious truth is that we were almost driven out of the country by ground squirrels.

I suppose I can be forgiven my one animal prejudice, since there was, after all, a bit of reason for it. But it was hard to forgive the prejudice against a lot of far nobler animals—the cougar, in particular. The cougar is one of the handsomest creatures on the continent. He stands about three feet high and gets perhaps three times that in length. He has a sleek, reddish-tan coat, and he is all suppleness and elegance. Not many people get to see the cougar in the wild, but this hasn't stopped a terrible campaign against him. Primarily because cougar do kill deer and sometimes calves, but more because they seem so fearsome in appearance, all states which have had them have had bounties on them of such size that for a long time there was a whole class of scruffy characters who called themselves hunters and lived by killing cougars. They are pretty much out of business now with changes in law, but there are still thousands of people who hate cougars.

A part of the trouble is that cougars look so wild, it's hard to believe they aren't appallingly dangerous. Most places, when word gets out that a cougar track has been seen, housewives shut themselves indoors and deputy sheriffs start oiling their guns. There are stories of cougar having killed humans. They are mostly lies. In truth, the cougar is a fairly timid and peaceable character who is also a good bit of a recluse. He lives off small animals and deer or a calf when cattle get too thick on the public domain. The cougar has to have a big country to survive in, so he covers a lot of territory. There are seldom many cougars in any one place. But some people will see a lynx track in the snow and report a cougar, terrifying the whole neighborhood.

There were, however, a good number of cougar in Stehekin when we first arrived. There had been a shortage of ammunition and a lack of hunters during the war, and the cat had multiplied in number along with the deer. Tracks were seen in the snow on the road, and we went down to look at them. They were impressive—six inches or more across. We heard that a number of cougar had been killed down by Domke Lake, but none in our valley. There was talk how somebody should go hunting.

That was about when Jane and Ray and I decided to go skiing up on the benches, where the snow was good. We had got up about five hundred feet above the valley, going along a little rocky spine first to one side and then the other. Ray, who was leading, stopped and said in a very casual voice,

"See that cougar over there?"

I looked across the valley, a mile or so. He couldn't be seeing even a moving cougar there. I said so.

"No, right there, by that tree."

I looked where he was pointing—it was just a few feet away from where we had come across the rock spine—and realized there was something peculiar about there being a rotted log not covered with snow when everything else was. The rotted log slowly stood up and revealed itself as a splendid cougar. He had been surprised, and with justified contempt for our powers of observation, had simply lain down. He looked at us for maybe thirty seconds, then silently leaped down the slope and vanished.

No one is entitled to such an experience twice, and it was not given us. We had only been three ski-lengths away, less than twenty feet. But we were aware of his presence—or maybe his mate's—through the winter. On one of those sunny days that come after a big storm, we built a fire of debris that had been accumulating in the woodshed—old cartons and the like—and watched it for a while before going in to lunch. When we came out to put the rest of the junk on the fire, we found a path beaten down into the snow around the fire, made by a cougar. We traced the track and found where he had been sitting under a tree, probably not very well hidden by a hump of snow. But according to the tracks, he had taken off in a long lope when we came back out. Several times after that we found his tracks between the house and the privy, but because we were through with our pyrotechnics, I suppose, he gave up on us.

Like other wild animals, cougar are curious. There are many stories of travellers in the hills who have for one reason or another turned back the way they had come and found tracks of a cougar who had been following them. Usually these stories are told with the shivery implication that the traveller had only luckily escaped with his life. And although this was clearly nonsense—the explanation being simple cat curiosity—the story usually ends with a great hue and cry and a big mobilization of deputy sheriffs.

We were awfully glad to see the particular tracks by the house, since they appeared after Ray had made his kill. That was earlier in the winter and we learned about it one night when the snow was falling heavily and we had gone down to call on the Courtneys. The whole family was in the front room. In the middle of the floor—it seemed to take up the entire floor space—was the body of a cougar. We fairly jumped back into the kitchen. Ray had stirred up old Beans, the family terrier-like mongrel who spent most of his time by the kitchen range, and the two of them had gone off to see if they couldn't get a cougar. The motive was simply the bounties paid by the state and the stockmen's association. And sure enough, old Beans had run after a cougar, who in the normal cougar way had climbed a tree. Ray shot it without difficulty.

So we sat for an hour admiring the cougar, beautiful and frightening even in death, and marvelling at the intrepid Beans, who now dozed modestly by the big heating stove in the corner. Finally, I saw a light come into Jane's eye.

"What are you going to do with the meat?" she asked.

There was deep silence for a moment or so. Finally, Hugh asked,

"Meat?"

"Yes," Jane said obliviously, "there's a lot of meat in that creature."

More silence. Then,

"Why, I don't know," Hugh said slowly. "Feed it to the dog, I guess."

The idea of old Beans making away with any significant portion of that carcass was absurd. Jane went on,

"Well, I've been reading the *Journals* of Lewis and Clark, and they say that their men found the two choicest delicacies they had were catamount and beaver tail. Catamount—that's cougar, and I'd like to try some."

There was another long silence and then somebody

changed the subject. As the snow was coming down pretty heavily, we went home soon.

Next morning, Ray came up to our house with a bundle. "I brought you a piece of that cougar."

We unwrapped it and there was a big roast about like a good sized ham. Jane remonstrated,

"Oh, this is wonderful. But you've given us too much. Your family should have it. I only wanted to try a bit of it. Won't your folks eat it?"

Ray shuffled nervously and said,

"Well, I guess not."

So we cooked the roast. The meat was, as Lewis and Clark had said, delicious. Underneath an inch of fat, the meat was very fine grained and delicate. It was white—something like pork—but much drier, and had a unique and subtle flavor. We shook our heads at the thought of most of it going to waste.

The next evening as we were turning to on the roast again, Ray appeared at the door. He sat down, after refusing to join us for dinner, and watched us eat for a while. Finally, he cleared his throat and said,

"Could I try just a bit of that meat?"

Gladly I cut him a slice. He picked up a fork, hesitated, then took a couple of bites. He nodded his head, put his fork down and said he had to get back home. We hadn't converted him, but all the same he had tried.

The following day was our turn to ski to the mail boat. The cougar kill had been made after the last boat and we looked forward to telling the story at the post office. But we didn't get to. We were given some funny looks as we came into the little waiting space, and somehow we couldn't get into our story. It turned out that everybody had already heard it, including our part in the affair. Actually, the way the story was told around the valley was that "the McConnells have been eating *cat.*" Our reputation had sunk out of sight.

It was the damned telephone, of course. If we had told it ourselves, leading up to it properly with Lewis and Clark and so on, maybe we might have put it in the right light. But we were too late, and maybe Lewis and Clark wouldn't have helped any more than they had with the Courtneys. It took quite a while before normal Stehekin tolerance began operating again and we were taken back into the community.

In due time, the Forest Service decided that since there hadn't been any big fires for a while, the phone line wasn't doing them much good. So they decided to get rid of it. They tried to sell it to Stehekin, but of course there wasn't any kind of organized body in Stehekin to sell it or give it to, and they tore it down.

This was the biggest technological advance ever made in Stehekin, I figured.

6.

Rather high on the list of deficiencies that downlake found in Stehekin was its absence of religion, or at any rate, of churches. Of course, there weren't enough people in the valley to support a regular church, but this was never really accepted as an excuse by the more determined evangelists who found their way up the lake from time to time.

You had to say these visitors tried. One of them was a relative of one of the older families of the valley. She had proved her mettle as a missionary in one of the darker parts of Africa. While on home leave, she proposed to carry her mission to Stehekin, which she plainly regarded as at least as benighted as her overseas post. She announced a prayer meeting to be held at the generally disused community hall. Word went around the valley that her local relatives would be very grateful to anyone who showed up. It was one of those appeals that go out when one of the neighbors needs help, as when Harry realized he did not have enough pickers for the apple harvest. There was quite a bit of grumbling, but a good part of the valley turned out for the meeting. In fact, the turnout was so good that the evangelist scheduled another meeting. But this time nobody except a couple of relatives came. It was a disaster that everyone wished for the sake of the family had not occurred, but there are limits to what could be endured, even for neighbors.

I suspect that this visitor returned to Africa with the bitter conclusion that she was going back to more fertile soil than the valley. This may or may not have been true, but it was not a necessary conclusion. She had simply come up against the Stehekin abhorrence of anything that was organized.

It does have to be said that Stehekin was a bit hard on preachers. Jack Blankenship, for example, typified the Stehekin attitude, which was that religion was a private affair and had nothing to do with churches or preachers. Actually, preachers were accepted like other folk—so long as they didn't act like preachers. One did retire to the end of the lake and he was as well liked by the valley as he liked the valley, which latter was probably because there wasn't any church. But back in the days when Jack had the old Golden West Lodge, the dining room there was the only place to get lunch if you came in on the boat. The boat would stop for two hours and the tourists would get out and file up the hill to the

110

hotel. As they would go into the dining room they would have to pass Jack, who stood in the doorway. Jack was big and he looked rough. If you looked at him you'd have to say he was the meanest looking man in the valley. It wasn't just that he scowled most of the time; it was the way he held himself with his thumbs hooked over his belt sagging down over his belly, and the way he growled when he talked. At first I wondered just how anybody could be as mean as he looked and sounded—then I discovered that nobody could, and that Jack wasn't. In fact, his appearance was all an act, but a stranger couldn't know this.

So when tourists came into the dining room at the Golden West, they quickly got an idea it was no place to make trouble, and their decorum was always excellent. But one day as the lunch crowd came quietly in past Jack, one little fellow hung back. After the crowd was pretty well through the door, he sidled up to Jack and asked in a very low voice,

"Are you the proprietor?"

"Yup," said Jack.

"Well," he said, clearing his voice a little uncertainly as he looked up at Jack, who was scowling as usual, "I don't know whether you are familiar with the custom outside. But it's usual at public establishments to give consideration to members of the clergy. I am pastor of. . . ."

His voice sort of trailed off as he felt Jack's eyes blazing down on him. And Jack just let him stand there for thirty seconds or so while the attention of the whole crowd got focused. Finally Jack said in a voice that shook the dining room,

"Well, God damn it, man, if you're broke, go on in and eat!"

Then Jack disappeared into the kitchen where he doubled over and tried to stifle his laughter.

Jack had been a sourdough during the great days of '98 in Alaska and had had his bout with mining fever. He never found anything in Alaska, but when he came to Stehekin as the first ranger for the U.S. Forest Service, he kept his eyes open for signs of minerals. And there were indeed such signs in most of the area; big streaks of reddish rocks denoting iron, and maybe, just maybe, deposits of more valuable mineral. The backwash from the Klondike brought dozens of would-be miners to pick over the most tantalizing spots. Even in the most forbidding places, one could find marks of long-past prospecting activity—tunnels running into the sides of cliffs for a hundred feet or so, and the remains of cabins crushed by the snows of many years and sinking into the ground as log by log they crumble in decay. Jack laid claim to some of the more remote of these "mines."

The mining laws of the United States date back to the nineteenth century, a time when they had a degree of appropriateness; but in their persistence, they amount to a curse upon the land. Though this is sometimes disputed by firms benefitting from the anachronism, it cannot be denied that the laws reflect a romanticism unparalleled in the statute books. For the slightest of investment—if one if lucky—it is possible to mark out a piece of ground and file a paper in the local county courthouse that gives you right to the minerals, provided only that you do a certain amount of work on the spot each year. Eventually, this can be converted to fee simple ownership of what had once been public land. The only other condition is that there must be a showing of mineral. Accordingly, the map of the North Cascades was pock-marked by numerous claims.

The claims that Jack had established, however, had never reached the stage of patenting, and indeed were in danger of lapsing for his failure to keep up with his yearly assessment work. Jack decided to restake his claims and asked me to go along to give a hand. We had a visitor who wanted to get into the hills and Jack was willing to have him go too. So Jack, Graham and I set off up the Agnes. We stopped the first night at Jack's lower cabin, a crumbling structure built out of big cedar logs at the foot of an unnamed peak. Rats ran over us all night and we were glad to get going the next morning. We went up a steep hillside into a hanging valley, wild except for the remains of an old trail. A mountain towered alongside us as we went and Jack said he had named it Needle Peak. It was a bad name, for it was more like a great cathedral dome, but Jack had placed so many names on points of the area that he had become careless and prosaic. He had started well, with Tupshin (the Arrow) for one mountain and Sandalee (roan colored) for the glacier with a pink fungus growing in it on the backside of McGregor. And, of course, he had named McGregor itself. But by the time he laid out the trail up the Agnes he had run dry. For example, he came to two creeks and decided one was to be Glacier Creek and the other Swamp Creek. But when the crew went up with the signs, they got mixed up and the signs were switched, and Jack never bothered to get them changed. So the maps got printed that way and officially we were now headed up Swamp Creek, which has no swamp in its entire length and starts from a good sized glacier. But I have never minded since the name has kept people out of that valley, and it's one of the finest things anywhere.

We reached Jack's upper cabin, which was too far disintegrated to sleep in, and went on to the claims. The first was in a cirque with a splendid waterfall coming down over the cliff at its head. As we approached, a goat ran behind the water fall and then took off across a cliff hanging on to nothing visible. The first claim was easy to get to; Jack found a couple of little tree trunks that had been broken off in a previous winter avalanche and we stuck those up at the lower corners of the claim. Then Jack took out the claim notice and put it in an empty Prince Albert tobacco can, which he nailed upside down to one of the posts. Jack always used Prince Albert cans and I gathered that it wouldn't be a legal posting if he used anything other than a PA can.

Then Jack led us off in the direction the goat had gone. There was a little ledge to walk along, and before long we were up a few hundred feet above the floor of the cirque. Jack stopped at the end of the ledge and pointed upward.

"You see that little bush growing out of that crack there?" he asked. "Now I want you fellows to climb up there and get me some ore samples."

It was awkward to get to—and exposed. However, Graham and I managed to get up by the little bush, and clung to it.

"All right now," said Jack, "one of you get up over there to the right and above a little ways. You'll see a little crack up a ways. That's got the ore. I'll pass one of you the pick."

It was touchy, but Graham managed to get where Jack had indicated and then Jack handed me the pick, and I was just barely able to reach over to Graham. Then Jack called again:

"No, damn it, not there—up over your head."

We were already in a precarious enough position, but with both of us edging along gingerly, trying to hold onto both the cliff and the pick, we got into position. I pushed against Graham's back to give him an illusion of security and he swung the pick over his head. With Jack's terse directions, he found the crack—a tiny crevice, actually. After an agonizingly long time, we had pried loose and caught maybe a coffee can full of dark rock. We climbed down. Back at the cabin, Jack picked over it and beamed.

"You see that there?" he asked. "That's galena; lead and silver. It's really rich."

Although no mining engineer from any big-time company before or after ever took an interest in the tiny amounts of mineral that could be located in any of Jack's claims, that fact never detracted from his pleasure in the rocks we brought back. He enjoyed showing them off at the lunch counter and he never let on that he had the slightest doubt about their commercial potential. The value of those rocks lay in the rationale they gave for regular trips to the spots where they were found. Any unbiased traveller would have to agree that the two valleys where he had his claims were about the wildest and most spectacular to be found.

From time to time Jack would hold forth at the lunch counter about his mines. He explained to any and all listeners that a long streak of rust-colored rock ran diagonally across the region. His claims, of course, were all in the center of this red band, "just like the Holden mine is." The lunch counter was the forum of Stehekin. Jack had built a handsome log structure for it and it was a warm and friendly place to be, especially during the hours after the boat had departed. The genius of the establishment was in the arrangement of the counter and its eighteen stools—a horseshoe which allowed everyone to join in whatever was being debated, and also to kid Beryl, who presided at the grill at the base. Actually, the latter was a bit risky, for she seldom returned less than she received. Like her husband, Jack, she had assumed the manner of a hard-bitten old-timer. One gradually learned that this was in good part an act, like Jack's, and the gamine of her true character appeared frequently.

By the time we arrived, Jack and Beryl had lost the Golden West through foreclosure of a mortgage for a few hundred dollars just when Beryl's daughter was dying, so she had some reason for her rough manner. But they had put themselves back together again, and Jack had managed to salvage another bit of property by the dock. On this property he built a building out of scrap lumber from the old Field Hotel, which had been razed when construction of a hydro plant at the foot of the lake raised the water level. This housed living quarters and the Post Office and stowage space for all the junk Jack had been collecting for two decades. The lunch counter came later, just after the end of World War II. In time the lunch counter became famous for the pie that Beryl made every day; it was sheer ambrosia. Crowds from the boat would jam the place each noon.

This was when Beryl's temperament showed. She would be working furiously, with a bit of hair dripping down over one eye, and somebody would get in her way, or a tourist sitting next to the grill would ask some damn fool question, and she would let go. Nobody could really blame her for telling the idiot off—nobody, that is, who watched for an hour or so

116

as we tended to do when we were down at the dock. Finally, she hit on a solution. Just as she was putting out a fire that had flared up in the grease on the griddle, a tourist innocently asked how high Rainbow Falls are. Instead of her usual snarl, she looked up, smiled sweetly and said:

"Fifteen hundred and thirty-six feet."

That's more than four times what they really are. Nevertheless, the tourist, who had just been to the falls, said thank you and walked out happily. It was the principle of the satisfying answer. It came to serve all of us well.

Beryl's father and brother also lived in Stehekin. The former, who was always known to everyone as Dad, was a small fellow possessed of amazing energy. He was one of the best square dancers in the valley and it was a fine sight to watch him dancing in the square with his great-granddaughter. He never seemed to grow any older than he was when we first saw him.

Her brother, Guy Imus, was the packer in the valley, and after Jack, the person who knew the vast back country best. Each year he would bring his horses uplake on a roundabout trail over one of the passes from their winter pastures and set about reinculcating in them some of the respect for the workaday world they had lost in their season of idleness. This process would involve Guy in fervent divine invocations, albeit in a spirit few preachers would approve. It wasn't that Guy really needed divine help in dealing with horses. He was a genuine expert and a marvel to be out with on the trail. Before he came to Stehekin he had been a member of what must have been the most elite group of specialists since the old-time Mississippi River pilots, the drivers of the twenty-four horse teams that pulled the big combines of the Big

Bend wheat country. Those teams are no more, and I suspect there aren't more than a couple of the drivers left alive. To see one of those outfits going over the skyline of the plateau above the Columbia was a glorious experience. The drivers were virtuosi—they had to be—and if they had a volatile temperament, as Guy definitely did, it was right and proper. Guy came to Stehekin as the horse began to disappear in the lowlands. He worked for a while at Holden and became something of an artist with dynamite. Whenever anybody in the valley wanted some blasting done, Guy was the man to get. His work was precise, efficient and beautiful to watch. There must have been some transfer from his work with horses.

One of the first of Guy's summer trips was always the circuit from Stehekin to Holden. This leads up the Agnes Creek Valley, a deep forested corridor that ascends gradually until the last few miles, where it rises rapidly toward the crest of the range. It is a sanctum in which one's step is muffled by the soft deposit of evergreen needles on the trail. The hush is accentuated by the low murmur of falling water, sometimes seen in the nearby creek but always sensed across the quiet. The valley is pristine save for the narrow span of the trail, and is something complete in itself. It is also the long prelude to the climax of Cloudy Pass.

In another time, Cloudy Pass could well have been regarded as the home of spirits. In good weather it's not dangerous, but rather a place of joy and wonder. During summer, flowers bloom everywhere, except where a snowbank fills the actual pass itself, and low, storm-twisted trees cover the hillside nearby. The land slopes gently toward the south into a large meadow that for several weeks is solid with color, first of the yellow glacier lilies, and then, after a pause, of all the varieties that occur in the high mountains. The meadow is known to its older habitués as North Star Park—named for the little peak rising above it, whose own name came about because from the most obvious camping spot below, the North Star appears directly above the peak's summit. The gentleness of North Star Park, however, is only noticeable after some time, for below and beyond it is a sight so dramatic that it commands first attention. This is Lyman Lake, lying in a broad cirque beneath a cluster of peaks. It is fed by a steep cascade flowing down through a series of pools linked directly to the snout of the Lyman Glacier, a smooth white expanse descending from the summit of Chiwawa, the most shapely of the peaks. To catalogue the parts in this manner, however, is to falsify: there is but a single whole, and the flowers of North Star Park are as much its essence as the rock and ice of Chiwawa.

A hundred feet to the north, a completely different vision appears. Off to the west, through the notch of Suiattle Pass a mile away, there is a sharp drop into dark forested depths. Above it, rising to an immense height, is the classic form of a volcano. Prosaically named Glacier Peak, it is entirely white. Despite the marks of great crevasses across its face, it gives such an impression of serenity that the contrast of the severe and the gentle so notable between the foreground and distance in the other view is exactly reversed here: the heights are gentle while the depths are stern.

A spot for rest and contemplation in good weather, Cloudy Pass nevertheless has reason for its name. When a storm from the Pacific advances on the range, all its violence seems bent on forcing its way through the pass. Then a cold wind rises up from the western canyons and a low cloud takes shape against the wall of the range. A tongue from it reaches up toward the pass, then over it and down to the Lyman cirque. Seen from below, it is a torrent falling into the cirque from some primordial source in the pass itself. Sometimes the cloudfall dissolves before it reaches North Star Park, but at other times it fills the entire basin; within seconds a violent blizzard may be raging. This can happen in any month of the year, although it is unlikely in July or August.

In April, when the snow lies twenty or more feet deep in North Star Park, such storms come and go quickly. A climb to the pass may start in a blinding sun that forces the shedding of every possible bit of clothing; just a few feet from the pass, however, a savagely cold wind can hit, bringing with it a blizzard that shuts out everything beyond the ski tips. But it is still worth pushing on to the summit. Even though Glacier Peak and Chiwawa may remain hidden, a break in the cloud may expose the ice-plastered cliffs of Fortress Mountain. Scored and fluted by nearly constant avalanches, it has become a Himalayan giant, austere and impossibly remote. At such moments a cluster of prayer flags in the pass would be fitting, tokens to the elements and reminders that men have come this way before.

Below and not too far away—two miles at most—and just beyond the lake, there was a haven, the Lyman Cabin. Built in 1926, when Lake Chelan's outlet was dammed so that electricity could be captured from the fall down to the Columbia, it served the snow survey team each spring—and anyone else who happened to know of its existence. In the eyes of purists it was inescapably an intrusion in a wilderness sanctuary; it nevertheless had a quality of belonging, for it was built from the greyed logs of the ghost forest around it. The forest itself was destroyed sometime in the eighteen nineties. Prospectors, greedily racing each other to discover the mineral that rumor and their own imaginations insisted had to exist but was hidden by the dense growth of the Railroad Creek Valley, simply set fire to the forest. It burned for weeks, its great pillar of smoke being seen by Mamie Courtney, then a child at Moore Point across Lake Chelan some twenty-five miles away. Nobody came to fight the fire and no penalties were visited on the arsonists. Fire was a recurrent feature of the forest; and if its cause was human, this was no less natural, it seemed, than if somehow lightning had reached down into the valley's depths. Perhaps there was truth in this perspective; at least by the test of lack of change, that part of nature which is human has continued to be as arrogant and destructive as it ever was.

Most of the valley forest was consumed entirely, but high up, the trees were sparse, and although they were killed, their trunks remained standing to shed their limbs and bark. A few still stand even today, with bare wood whitened by storm and sun, wraiths of ancient splendor towering above the new growth of conifers now slowly reaching out above the protective first cover of willow and alder.

The interior of the cabin was just big enough to accommodate a pair of double bunks, a home-made table with a couple of benches, and a decidedly cobbled-up stove. The last was intended to serve the double purposes of heating and cooking, but did neither well, taking too much wood for cooking and yielding heat too stingily. In order to cook on its surface, such a roaring fire had to be coaxed from the rather poor wood available until the sides glowed red and approach to it was a blistering experience. Nonetheless, the cabin was a marvel of comfort and security, especially during the storms of winter—if it could be found. Although it was located on a slope and the steep pitched roof at the lower end was high above ground, the snow would often bury it completely. One might know precisely the location of the little glade where it stood, and still have to search for a half hour to find the cabin. But if all went well and the blizzard was not too intense, a gray pole sticking a foot or so above the snow would resolve itself into something unnatural. Examination would reveal a pulley with a rope running over it. The rope would lead a foot or so down to the handle of a shovel which, once freed from the snow and ice, became the key to warmth, food and all the joys of safety and animal comfort. First of all, however, the shovel had to be used to dig down to the door and clear a passage so the stovepipe could be connected to the stove and led up to air. It took a while, and made for a certain appreciation of the shelter when it was achieved.

Ordinarily—other than during the summer hiking season, that is—there was little reason to expect that anyone else would turn up at the Lyman Cabin to share its tight quarters. Hunters might stray into it, but usually they were not this enterprising; and by the time the fall storms began, it stood deserted and unused. This was the time, however, when it had to be made ready for winter and the coming of the snow survey party for which it was built, the stovepipe dismantled and piled inside, wood cut for a few days' use and some extra in case of a protracted storm, and food cached inside. In the past, all these things could be done at any time with certainty that the arrangements would be respected by anyone who turned up; even kindling could be left piled beside the stove with confidence that if it were used it would be fully replaced. The decline of the custom of leaving enough wood and kindling in a protected place by a campsite or cabin is perhaps a measure of the change that has come to the wild places of America, but at any rate, it has not entirely disappeared in the Cascades. Nevertheless, things had changed enough even then that stocking the Lyman Cabin was best done after the hunting season.

So late one year a while back, Guy went up the Agnes and over Cloudy with a couple of horse loads for Lyman. The weather was not good and some snow had already fallen. He had got in during the early afternoon and, sensing the probability of a storm—perhaps the last through which it might be possible to get horses back over the pass for the year—he turned to and managed to get enough wood cut. As it grew dark, the storm arrived; and he settled in the cabin for the night, hoping that things would not be too bad for the return to Stehekin the next day.

He was cooking supper and probably had been making the ordinary sounds that go with that operation when something prompted him to open the door of the cabin, although he wasn't conscious of any noise outside. There, just a few inches from his own face, was a man. The dim light from the kerosene lamp flickered as a blast of wind swept inside. It was all but impossible to make out any features on the face outside.

"What in . . ." Guy started.

Abruptly the figure turned and vanished into the darkness. Guy finally called a couple of times, but the wind threw his words back. After a few moments, he shut the door. There was no reappearance of the apparition, though Guy slept fitfully through most of the night.

The trip back over the pass and down to Stehekin the next day was a mean one and a long one, rather more than thirty miles. The weather was bad, and stopping to rest was even more unpleasant than going on. And there was the nagging thought of the visitor of the night before. It was not a good time for anyone to be alone in the hills. At least two deaths had occurred in the vicinity of Cloudy. There was the fellow who had been trapping one winter up Railroad Creek. He didn't come back from one of his trips up the valley. His body was found in the summer, when somebody poked into an old tunnel a prospector had drilled fifty feet or so into the rock alongside the trail just where it pulls up over the last step of the valley toward Lyman cirque. Then there was the Mexican who quit a trail crew up in North Star Park and headed back over the pass toward Stehekin. He had got his directions wrong, probably from difficulty with the language, and instead of going down the Agnes from the junction, had gone up to Suiattle Pass and got caught in a snowstorm. This was on the first of September and the snow went quickly. His body was found on the trail a few days later when a late party came through. It wasn't good to think of somebody back up there alone.

It had to be Blue Mountain Ole. There wasn't anybody else—aside from Guy himself—who would be at Lyman in late fall, or who would behave like that. Blue Mountain Ole actually had a cabin of his own up there—or shelter, rather—and he was always alone; nobody ever came with him. Supposedly, he had a "mine," and he wouldn't tell anybody where it was. Guy was pretty sure there wasn't any claim, let alone any ore body. For that matter, there wasn't even anything named Blue Mountain in the area. Ole's nickname came from the fact that there was a peak called *Red* Mountain near Chiwawa. There was a mine there (of generally the same sort as the others) and one of the men there was also named Ole, and he got to being called Red Mountain Ole. So it was entirely natural that the second Ole got called Blue Mountain Ole. Or maybe he was really the first Ole and somehow he got his nickname because he passed up Red Mountain and went over Phelps Pass, a wild little gap alongside Chiwawa, and came on over to the Lyman cirque.

Whether Blue Mountain Ole had actually found anything in the way of minerals still isn't clear, and it doesn't seem to matter. Probably not, first because the area has been pretty thoroughly prospected over the years and nothing worthwhile has been found, but more because of the location of his cabin. Its site was just below Phelps Pass and above timberline, quite a few hundred feet higher than the Lyman Cabin, in fact. It was on a little grassy meadow—grassy, that is, for the couple of months it wasn't under snow—and just a few hundred feet from the edge of the Lyman Glacier as it used to be. The glacier has now receded nearly a mile since the first extant picture was taken of it early in the century, and there is quite a distance to the glacier from where the cabin stood. But the cabin was built a long time ago, out of the same fire-ravaged ghost stand as the Lyman Cabin, and when I first saw it, the lower logs had already rotted away and the whole structure was sinking into the earth. The top of the doorway was only about three feet above ground, and most of the shakes had caved in or blown away. It was just a matter of time before the only sign of former human presence would be a rectangular outline of rotted wood level with the ground. You see these outlines from time to time if you wander in the hills, and wonder just what impulse led humans to locate in such spots.

With Blue Mountain Ole's cabin, however, the answer was plain. It was on just about the wildest and most exquisite spot that could be found. Standing in front of the door—or within it when that was possible—you looked right up the sweep of the glacier to the peak of Chiwawa with its usual banner of clouds flying from the summit. It was austere in the extreme, and most of the local people would have only contempt for the choice of a location so exposed, unprotected, and far from a good supply of wood. Even the door faced directly into the prevailing storms. In every sense, it defied practicality. So the secret of Blue Mountain Ole's mine had to be right there; his "claim" was not to some hypothetical body of minerals but to the spot the cabin stood on.

Down nine miles from the Lyman cabin was a real mine, the Holden mine. This, like the "mines" that had been staked early in the century, had seen a succession of wild hopes and wilder plans like the one that gave its valley its name, Railroad Creek. In 1937, however, a large crew arrived and began the building of a road up the valley, a large camp and a mill. Miners set to tunneling into the flank of a sharp peak to expose a large body of low grade ore containing copper and small amounts of other minerals, including some gold. And the mine actually went into production, with concentrated ore being trucked down to Lake Chelan, then barged to Chelan and re-trucked to the railroad alongside the Columbia. The large mining company that invested the money boasted that it had enough minerals to last the operation twenty years.

The town of Chelan, which had been bragging about the riches buried in this hinterland and hoping for its development, now began to have second thoughts about the actuality. For the first time, it conceived dire pictures of what might happen to law and order in its quiet streets and particularly to its wives and daughters. The first big holiday for the miners would be the Fourth of July, and they were being given time off for the celebration downlake. The local paper told of preparations being frantically made for the feared disturbances when the miners came to town, primarily the hiring of additional police. In the mining camp these preparations were greeted with derision and indignation. And, by common consent, the miners chartered an airplane and flew off to San Francisco. Chelan had a safe and sane (if disappointing) Fourth; San Francisco somehow survived.

With time, however, everyone relaxed, since the mining camp blossomed into a neat little company town with families living there and order well kept. It does have to be said, though, that not all the miners were family men. For these, there were dormitories built by the company. For recreation, there were movies and occasionally live entertainers. More important, there was the little village of Lucerne (not established by the company) at the mouth of Railroad Creek on Lake Chelan. Lucerne offered more robust entertainments, including a tavern. There was also an amusement park that some entrepreneur had started up on a promontory a half mile or so up the lake from Lucerne. It never appeared on any map. Locally, however, it was well and affectionately known as Pecker Point.

With the passage of time, however, virtue and religion won out. In 1957, the mining company forecast of a twenty-year life for the mine was realized. An accident inside the labyrinth of tunnels let loose a torrent of ground tailings and water that had been pumped into the disused tunnels to help prop the mountain up. And although much ore was still left, the mine shut down for good. The village of family houses was erased, leaving only the dormitories and the dining hall. With the miners gone, the Forest Service sold the remaining buildings for a summer camp. The buyer was the Lutheran Church.

7.

There is a dream which I think anyone who has lived where water is scarce must at some time have shared. It is the vision of a small stream of clear, clear water, bubbling and murmuring over a bed of clean, washed gravel. It is only a foot or two wide and not more than six inches deep. But its water is cold and sweet and it runs down through the front yard, say thirty feet or so from the door of the cabin. Its course isn't straight; it twists and turns irregularly, giving life to the soft grass and bushes by its sides. Its water is easily diverted indoors by a pipe laid into the stream a short distance above the cabin. It never dries up, even in the hottest summers. On the most blistering days of July and August, it has enough force to run a high-spraying sprinkler which wets down the grass by the door and cools the air near the cabin.

It's a common enough picture. Almost everyone who has wandered through the mountain foothills has seen such favored sights. Through the years that we lived in Stehekin, I had this dream with annoying frequency, and I used to scheme and make grandiose plans by which I could bring this sight to reality before our house.

The Cascades are, above all, well-watered mountains. During the winter months, the storms of the Pacific sweep in from their birthplace in the Gulf of Alaska. They drench the western slope of the range with rains that in places leave a hundred inches of water each year. On the crests and down to the four thousand foot level, and sometimes even lower, the snow piles deep and lasts for half the year. In the higher elevations, the snow never disappears. It is blown by winds and avalanched into the canyons where the glaciers lie, and these are renewed, now to advance, now to recede, but never to disappear. On the high wooded hills the trees and brush shade the ground, and the duff of centuries holds the moisture so that constantly, throughout each year, it seeps downward to bubble out in springs and trickling streams. In the valleys below the glaciers, there are always bright sparkling creeks, and often rivers.

On the eastern slopes of the range, however, the hills grow dry, the streams thin, and finally, where the land levels out, there are only sagebrush and dusty waterless gullies. The precipitation here is often as little as eight inches in a year. The Stehekin Valley is midway between these extremes, partaking from year to year of the characteristics now of the west, now of the east. The forests of the valley are a mixture of east and west. Where the sun shines hottest, there are pines; where there is frequent shadow, there are firs. Often the line that separates these western and eastern species is devious and discontinuous. But the two types are constant reminders that this is the boundary between the humid and the arid lands of the west.

From midsummer through September, however, it seems that this is an eastern valley. The twigs and needles on the ground snap, and the dirt in the trail is a powder that flies into the air when touched. These were the months when I most often fell to speculating about how to bring that little stream bubbling past the house.

The water system that we had built was one of Curt's engineering. It involved a nine-hundred-foot pipeline from the river to a wooden storage tank on a rock behind the house, and a little gasoline-driven centrifugal pump. The plan was actually much more complex than this bare outline suggests, and I am sure that Curt was delighted with its very complexity. It worked, too. That is, it worked provided the pump engine could be started. I was assured by many self-certified experts that this engine was the quintessence of simplicity, but years of experience taught me better. There were moments when I would approach the thing whistling, with nothing on my mind; would flip the choke carelessly, curl the starting rope around its flywheel and pull. It would purr into instant and furious activity. Water would gush up the pipe and in an hour my tank would be overflowing.

More frequently, however, I would adjust the choke carefully, fix the rope, and yank. Nothing would happen. Six more yanks of the rope, though perhaps with a little more strength, and still nothing would happen. Twenty more yanks would give me only a sore arm. Or maybe on the twentieth yank, the flywheel would come loose and I would have to struggle to get it back on. And there were other pieces that could come loose. I'd tell myself that my patience was infinite, would work carefully and precisely to get the parts all in their appointed order, and try again. Nothing would happen. It was just too much for my temper. I swore. I threatened it with a pipe-wrench, a hammer, a rock, anything that was at hand. And often this worked. One more pull and the thing would start.

It was a device to make any man superstitious. No rational explanation was possible for either its starts or its refusals. On the mornings on which I knew I would have to refill the tank, I'd lie in bed longer than usual. At first, it was to give me time to think out some workable approach to the problem. The only idea that ever came to me, however, was that I should take a different route to the river, creeping from tree to tree until I was upon the thing, and pull the rope before it knew I was anywhere about. I know that it would have ended in breaking my spirit utterly if in one final rage I had not renounced the system completely and built a different system, one that led the water from a spring on the hill down to the house by gravity. Curt, I know, was hurt by my ultimate rejection of his finely engineered plan. He had been called in often to work on the pump. At first, he had only to smile and pull the rope once. The thing would start. These were moments when my heart welled with hatred. But Curt came a few times too often. He began to receive my usual treatment. It was my turn to smile. I might be without water, but the strain on Curt's belief in the rationality of machinery was balm to my malice. Curt's faith never gave way, though, and ultimately—by his sheer persistence and the laws of chance, I am convinced—the engine would start. In the end, however, I had my full revenge on Curt for his patient explanations of the beauty of machines. I gave him the pump and its engine. Somehow we remained friends.

And so, each year as the spring faded into summer, I'd daydream of that little brook that would bubble down by the house. The dream went on until the year of '48. The winter had been heavy, although not remarkably so; the two winters before it had been as heavy. The March snow survey showed a large amount of snow with a fairly high water content. The figures were not alarming, and I think few people other than engineers and statisticians paid them much attention.

But the winter would not end. Usually after the middle of February there is little new snow. There are storms, but these are brief; the snows they leave are, except in the high country, insignificant flurries that do not add to the snow depth. During February, the days grow markedly longer and the sun is out strong and bright, so strong that a good sunburn is the result of being out too long. It is a good time, one when the snow softens during the day but hardens at night, and when the sap rises almost visibly in the maples and one is tempted to catch some of it in buckets. March is apt to be stormier, but only fitfully; its snows are inconsequential despite the frequently darkened days.

In '48, February and March came as usual. But April never appeared. April is the month when the sun grows brilliant and powerful and the water comes off the hills in torrents, glistening like so much of the sunlight that brought it down.

But April this year was dark. Storm followed storm with almost no break. Each day was gloomy, and a cloud seemed perpetually to hang in the valley. The river, which each day I expected to see rising in its banks, stayed low. The anchor ice, the ice that forms at the bottom of the river while the fast-paced current rushes over it, disappeared. But otherwise, winter remained. The buds which had appeared in February and had grown during March suspended their growth. We wondered what was going on in the high country.

We took a trip up the valley. Each mile told some of the story. Just above us a bit, the snow was not only not melting, it was deepening. People in the valley shook their heads; this could not be. Even though there was not much run-off, the snow should sink under its own weight and get lower. Word came of a late snow survey made on the eastern side near the end of April. The snow by actual measurement *had* deepened through both March and April. No one needed to be told that this meant heavy new snow, for any gain in depth would have to counter the effect of settling. And we were not surprised to learn that the water content was extremely high.

Gradually, the snow did go out of the valley, and the road opened near the middle of what by the calendar was April. Clouds hid the hills so that we could see little above the valley floor. But everyone knew what lay above us, still growing, poised more and more precariously and, each day, each night, more ominously.

May appeared on the calendar, but it might have been early March. The glacier lilies came up and with them the spring beauties, as though they would be denied no longer. Several rains came, but they were cold. I watched the river; it showed scarcely any effect. It went up slightly after the rain began and dropped almost as soon as the storm had passed. Usually, in spring or summer, the full effect of a rain shows in the river eight hours after the height of the storm. These rains, up high, were not rain, but snow.

The deer stayed in the valley longer than usual. Normally, their migration can be plotted day by day as they move along the shores of the lake and on up the valley to their routes into the uplands. By twos, by threes, by groups of a half dozen they were everywhere in the valley for weeks. They, too, were waiting.

This was the year the bridge was to be finished. Nearly everyone in the valley was involved in the project in one way or another, although not everyone was anxious to see the bridge go in. We had chosen the western side of the valley because it, unlike its opposite, was free of rattlesnakes. What accounts for this rigid observance of this boundary by the snakes I have never learned, but it is one which can be counted on. The snakes seem never to have crossed either the old bridge or the new. The old bridge was one that they might have regarded with mistrust; nearly everyone but Curt and we did so.

The old bridge was actually the third that had stood in its location, but it was by far the noblest in its line. The Forest Service had been the responsible authority, but obviously none of the government's engineers had been allowed to learn of the undertaking. It had been built with complete contempt for the arts and crafts of the slide-rule clan. When the previous bridge went down the river, the district ranger came and shook his head at the site. He scratched with his pencil and then shook his head some more. The fact of the matter was that the Forest Service in Stehekin was in financially straitened circumstances. The timber of the valley had never struck the Service as having much value, so why should any great amount of the public monies be squandered where there was nothing but mountains? Still, the ranger at the head of the lake felt a responsibility.

"Harry," he asked Harry Buckner as both stood gazing at the site of the vanished bridge, "do you think we could build a bridge here for $600?"

"I don't know about the Forest Service," Harry replied, "but us farmers could."

"Well, that's what I've got left this year. Let's try."

And so it was done. The $600 wasn't enough by almost half, but the bridge was built. Harry had carefully failed to tell the ranger that the bridge which had disappeared had been privately built, and the ranger had not asked. The matter of design was also not questioned. Tall trees grew close by. Seven of them were felled, stripped of their boughs and bark and then hoisted onto two piers. The thing was decked over and two plank tracks were laid on for appearances.

It was a marvelous structure. The span was more than one hundred feet, all of it over rushing water. There was probably a time after it was first built in 1926 when it stretched straight and true across the water. But even the toughest of mountain fir was not made to be this unyielding for long. Gradually over the years a sag developed in the span. When I first saw it in 1937 it was a rather gentle, although already pronounced, dip. Steadily, this became a deeper and deeper catenary. By the winter of 1947 and 1948, the dip was just great enough that when one crossed it on skis, there was a soft free ride to the middle and halfway uphill. A companion skiing ahead onto it would suddenly disappear in the sag, then spurt into sight a second later.

As the years went by, my fondness for that bridge grew. Once a creation of man, straight and uncompromising as no thing of nature ever could be, it fitted itself into the country out of which its materials had been hewn. It became a thing of grace. Its logs turned gray and mellow and they throbbed with the life of the waters below.

But there were those who did not share my pleasure in the bridge, including, in fact, almost everybody who saw it. Much of their attitude has to be set down to prejudice. By 1944, some visiting high official of the Forest Service had taken one look at it and ordered a sign put up. That sign was there and fading several years later. In crude and hurried lettering, it read: "Bridge Unsafe. Do not cross." As if this were not prejudicial enough, it was later joined by a more formally lettered board: "Bridge Condemned." But there are many officials of high standing in the government, so still a third sign was added after another couple of years: "Bridge Closed." Nothing more was done for a year after that, but we were at least assured that officialdom, though its life may consist of words and directives, does not reside in offices alone. And the signs did give a certain flavor to the scene, standing beside the bridge with the current of the Stehekin swirling a few feet below and the bridge itself gently pulsing to the river's motion, undisturbed, triumphant and serene.

Sometimes in a moment of malice when we had a susceptible visitor along, I used to enjoy stopping the old command car by those signs, then walking out onto the span. I would kneel and look down at the water, then return thoughtfully to the car and drive across in silence. This was sufficient for most guests. Once, however, I overdid it. I took out my pocket knife and poked its blade at the topmost stringer. It disappeared halfway into the log with no effort at all.

Ultimately and sadly, I joined with those who said that we must have a new bridge. There were long and involved parleys with officialdom. Finally, an excuse was found in some obscure legislation, and the decision was made to build a new bridge. But this time there would be no slipshod work. The engineers would have their way. They designed a textbook structure with overhead supports, beams striking at precisely proper angles and stresses placed just so. It was built from alien timbers sawed someplace in Oregon and impregnated with an ugly metallic green. The bill for this masterpiece of science, we were told, was upwards from $50,000.

Preparations for the new bridge proceeded slowly, but were well started when officialdom arrived again. The new site must be moved twenty more feet upstream. The delay meant that by the spring of '48, the new bridge—which should have been completed and in use the year before—was standing stark and angular upon two pedestals seemingly not far from midstream. The thing could be reached by a long ladder placed against one end, and I was rather glad that this was possible; for this high platform was an exhilarating vantage point from which to watch the last ordeal of my old friend below.

So, as the first days of May came in '48 and the weather continued cold and blustery, with acres of water hanging above us, we thought often of the old swayback bridge. This would be the end, and we grieved each day we passed over its lovely inverted arc.

But day by day the moment held off. There were rifts in the clouds now, and we could see the snow on the tops and shoulders of McGregor, Rainbow, and Sisi Ridge. Blackberry Mountain had deep snow well down into the usually empty cirque in its side. The wind that opened the clouds remained cold. There had been no chinooks since January, yet this wind of May was a wind of winter. The river remained constant, clear, and low.

The first week of May passed as though it were the first of March. The second week began the same way, and wore on, still cold. The tenth of May, the eleventh, the twelfth—all were chill and raw.

On the thirteenth a change took place. The sky was cloudless for almost the first time since February. The peaks glittered with a brilliance that I had quite forgotten. At eight in the morning the temperature was sixty-two degrees. No wind. I looked about and saw life everywhere—the life of birds in the air, squirrels in the trees, ants and insects on the ground, bright green shoots in almost visible motion in the earth. And water on the hills.

It could not really be seen at a distance, but it was unmistakable. There was the sound. The roar of the river has many pitches, but for months it had been constant. Now it was different. The sound was louder. It wasn't a big change, but it was there.

Sometime during the night, probably about two in the morning, a new mass of air arrived over the Cascades. Softly it settled on the peaks and tumbled into the basins; it flowed into the valleys and spring had come. In Cascade Pass and Suiattle Pass, on Bonanza and Booker, on McGregor and McAlester, in Horseshoe Basin, at Cedar, Hemlock, and Cottonwood Camps, on Crocker, Sulphide, and Horsefly cabins, on hundreds of ridges and thousands of gullies, the snow settled and its crystals collapsed. Water dripped from icicles high on the rocks of Logan; it dripped from the trees at the crest of Cloudy Pass and on Rainy Pass. It moved in runnels on the surface of the Sandalee Glacier and the great Chickamin itself.

All plans for the day forgotten, we jumped into the car and headed up the valley for a look at the spring from a height. We paused by the junction of the Agnes and the Stehekin and looked up toward the snowclad crags of the Agnes Range. The ice was already off the triangular face of Agnes Peak, but everywhere else was white. The face of Chickamin Glacier glistened moistly. And below us the Agnes was flowing with an opaque and muddy current, mingling its waters with those of the still-clear Stehekin.

We set off up the hot slope of Junction Mountain. Five hundred feet up we found the deer again. They were on the move now, heading upward to the crests of the ridges and the green and hidden meadows where they would stay until fall. They were everywhere—browsing quietly, watching us, but moving steadily and purposefully upward.

The sun grew hot and the earth of the steep slope dried as we watched. Over the rocks the heat rose in waves and, when we pushed too hard, too long, we were sickened. The chaparral curled in the heat and the air was pungent with its oppressive odor. From the six-thousand-foot summit, we looked out into the valleys and basins; all of them, even the lowest, held snow, deep snow.

We were back in the valley by mid-afternoon. It was echoing with a tumult of sound now. The Agnes was furious, pouring a torrent into the Stehekin. The waters of the two streams were now indistinguishable. Those of the Stehekin were as clouded as those of the Agnes, and both were darker than I had seen either before.

Across the road, little streams by the dozen were cutting their way into the dirt. Pools were standing in the hollows, and new waterfalls fell everywhere from the cliffs. Beside us the river flew by with an implacable fury. With foresight of what was to come, I left the car on the east side of the river and we took the trolley across. The trolley was an invaluable device, a simple wood platform suspended from pulleys that traveled on a cable stretched between two trees on opposite sides of the stream. The ground trembled as we approached the river and climbed up to the trolley. Below us, we could hear the great granite boulders of the river bed rolling and grinding. And on the rock I had been watching each day for weeks now, the river had risen three feet since morning.

At four-thirty that afternoon the temperature was ninety. And all through the night it remained warm. The sounds of the river steadily grew louder until I drifted into a fitful sleep.

In the morning, I found that my daydream of years had come true. There was a new little stream coming out of the woods from back of the woodshed and meandering past the house. It had fashioned a little channel for itself and already had a bed of clean washed gravel. It was cold and clear. I dipped my hands in it and wondered.

That day was like its predecessor: sunny, brilliant, and hot. A light haze developed in the greatest heat of the afternoon and the mountains seemed to grow more remote. But each hour the river was higher. We could hardly move from its side. As we watched, it cut into an old channel across from us and the land which had been the other side became an island. Small trees were coming down now, riding the current as though driven by a typhoon. Back at the house, my little stream had become a creek. I seized a shovel and worked furiously. Finally the angry little current turned away from the house foundations.

The third day, too, was warm, but it was different. The haze had completely gone. Something had occurred in the air making it clearer than I had ever known air to be. It was a magnifying glass that brought the mountains close, so close that they hung over us. McGregor's summit grew in height as we watched. The sky became a deep, deep blue that seemed unreal. It was as though the river, the mountains, the sun, and the sky had entered into some great contest whose goal was sheer abstract intensity.

Then toward evening, the first thunderhead appeared above the ridge of McGregor. It rose higher and higher until it covered half our narrow arc of sky. Others appeared from behind Rainbow Mountain and Sisi Ridge. Briefly, they were white; then they began to darken, and by sunset the sky was a solid dark boiling mass.

It was night when the lightning appeared. Thunder joined the roar of the river, and then the rain began. It came down furiously for perhaps an hour, then the thunder rolled away to some more distant ranges. But the rain continued through the night. It was not, after the first few hours, the hard driving rain of the thunderstorm, but the steady, strong, and determined rain of the two months when there had been only squalls. And it was warm. It melted the snows with a swiftness that not even the sun of the days before had been able to attain.

The river reached a height that day that had not before in the short memory of man been matched. The Stehekin, for all its obscurity and despite its short length—little more than twenty-three miles—is one of the dramatic streams of the land. It starts from a dozen or more glaciers and tumbles furiously through jagged mountains into the great chasm of its valley and Lake Chelan. Near the end of autumn, when the snows have gone except for those which are sinking into the ice of the Chickamin and other glaciers, its stream is thin and narrow. In late October, it flows at the rate of 125 cubic feet per second. In normal high water, usually in the third week of May, it runs at 11,000 cubic feet per second. During the flood of '48 it hopelessly overran the gauges, but the engineer's estimate is that its flow was 18,000 cubic feet per second.

As I watched it at its height, it was an awesome sight. Trees and logs were everywhere. The rain was coming down through a low-hanging cloud and a light fog rose from the river. Its expanse, now four or five times what it had been, was ominous, and the scene, unlike that of the day before, was somber, oppressive and menacing.

The bridge, the old swayback, was gone now. It went sometime during the night while nobody was watching. Harry had stood by its approach near evening the day before, just as the rains began. He had seen it quiver under the incessant battering of logs and floating trees. Several inches of water were flowing over its decking, but still it stayed. Once, he had held his breath as he saw a giant cottonwood careening down the current. It was a heavy, massive thing, traveling with all the force of the river. Its dense shallow root structure rode high in the air and caught near the end of the bridge, and the mass of the trunk swung hard against the deepest dip of the bridge. For a moment the cottonwood hung there and the bridge trembled violently. Then the current forced the trunk beneath the surface, and the whole tree vanished under the bridge, which still stood. Harry went home then, thinking that the bridge would have to be dynamited in the end.

But it was not to be by such an indignity that it went. The rise of the night took it out. We learned how it had been a number of days later. Someone exploring after the flood had receded a bit found the bridge intact, miles down from where it had stood. The rising water had simply lifted it off its piers and floated it away.

This, then, was our world. We were isolated from the other side of the river and the road. The trolley, too, had gone, its cable snagged by the roots of a passing tree. The radio brought the news that the storm had struck everywhere in the northwest. The Clark's Fork, the Okanogan, the Methow, the Entiat, the Yakima, the Klickitat, the Columbia, every mountain-fed stream of the region was in flood with the late-held snows. Ranches were destroyed, houses washed away, roads demolished, and lives taken. Downstream, the Columbia erased a whole town that had been built for shipbuilders in the late war. It was a national disaster.

We could vaguely picture these events elsewhere, and we could sympathize. But it was difficult to believe that there had been any force in nature left over from what we had seen ourselves. Ours had been the real event, the real flood, and it was hard to realize that the world was wider than what lay before our eyes.

8.

The roots of change must have got their start during World War II, although it wasn't apparent until quite a bit later. You wouldn't think the war would affect Stehekin, but it did—in several ways. In the first place, the government, which in a technical sense owned most of the area, more or less moved out. There had been a Forest Service ranger station and a couple of guard stations at Stehekin, occupied by a succession of men working for that bureau. But with the war, the Forest Service got short-handed, so they abandoned the area and moved downlake to Chelan, where things were more comfortable. Anyhow, Stehekin was too worthless to bother with. As one ranger put it a few years later, you couldn't grow much of anything there. And the timber was too tough; it would dull a saw in no time, and if you tried to put a sixteen-penny nail through a dry two-by-four cut in Stehekin you'd have to give up unless you had a drill handy.

Now this wasn't too bad a change—in fact, it wasn't much of a change at all. Most of what the Forest Service did at that time in Stehekin came under their heading of "fire-suppression"; that is, they kept open a number of trails, put lookouts on a few high points and issued fire permits for travellers (I rather used to enjoy going in to one of their stations and asking for a forest-fire permit). Maybe they put out some fires that might have gotten big, but Ray thought not; almost all fires were in old snags hit by lightning way up on the ridges where there wasn't much else to burn. The one fire that did get going during that era was on Junction Mountain in 1940, and it was rain that ultimately did that one in. All the same, it seemed like a good idea to have somebody on hand organized to fight fire. And to read or hear about the Forest Service putting out forest fires was what it was all about; their symbol was Smokey the Bear.

The other change was a lot more serious. Ray and Curt got drafted. Laurence was let off because he had chopped off a thumb while splitting wood years before. But Ray and Curt were taken. Curt got upset about it, partly because he hated the thought of being asked to do any killing, but also because he didn't see how his folks, who were aging, could get along without help from him and his brothers. So he went down to Wenatchee where the draft board lived and told them he was needed at home. The draft board asked him how much cash the family needed to live on for a year and Curt told them a few hundred dollars. At that they replied Curt would be sending home an allotment from his pay for a lot more than that, and he was in the army.

So, while Laurence went out to drive a truck, Ray went off to various places with the army and wound up running a saw-mill in the Philippines. Curt's military career was shorter but it was also glorious in its way. He got shipped up on a mission to throw the enemy out of Kiska in the Aleutians. He didn't like it, especially the seasickness, but fortunately the enemy had pulled out leaving most of their stuff on the island. I can imagine that the army had done its best to make Curt a proper military figure, but instead, he came close to Stehekinizing his part of the army. He was miserable sleeping out in the wet of the island, but it wasn't so much the cold and the wet, actually, as it was the blue fox that kept crawling into his sleeping bag. There had been a fox farm on the island before it was taken and the foxes had gone wild. Certainly Curt was wild trying to deal with a blue fox in one of those little army sleeping bags. This was enough and Curt took measures.

Since everybody else was feeling low with the cold and the wet and the darkness and since this included the officers, Curt got word through the top sergeant to the general that he might be able to get the camp some electricity if he could have some help hauling things from the enemy dump where he had been poking around. So he led a detail down and hauled up a disabled generator and dismounted the engine from a Japanese truck. Both were much better than anything that was ever found in the Stehekin dump, and Curt soon had lights rigged to the general's tent. The general then saw to it that Curt had one of the few big sixteen-man tents all to himself and the light plant, and he issued orders to the sergeant not to bother Curt. So Curt sat warm and dry with coffee going continually on top of the engine and served pancakes to his buddies all day. This didn't set too well with the rest of the army, so they used his bad back as reason for a discharge. Curt collected himself some souvenirs like spark plugs and other parts from the Japanese dump that might come in handy at Stehekin and came home.

This might seem no more than an interlude in the life of Stehekin, and a small one at that, but it turned out to have consequences. The first was the little house he built—his first, and the one that Jane ultimately bought from him for the two of us. He had started it before going to war, and had already decided it would have to be like the houses in Wenatchee and other big cities he had visited. It wouldn't be like his folks' log cabin, which was the most beautiful building ever put up in the valley. No, it would be modern and built of lumber. When he came back he hired Andy to put in wallpaper with flowers and leaves all over it. But that was just one sign of something more general: Curt had seen a lot of the downlake world by the time he came back, and he saw just how far behind Stehekin was.

It wasn't that Curt actually thought downlake was better, with its army and all the rest. Sitting there in his big tent with the generator on Kiska and feeding his buddies pancakes, he heard enough from them to know better. Just about all of them were miserable in one way or another. They didn't like where they were just then, of course, but they hadn't liked the lives they had led before getting into the army either, and they dreaded going back even though that would mean they'd be out of the army. Curt listened to them, and probably gave them a lot of help just by doing that. Then he got to talking about Stehekin. I'm sure he didn't mean to mislead any of them. But he was always an optimist, and he inherited his father's gift of telling stories. Above all, he had lived all his life in Stehekin and had the valley's way of looking at things.

You can just see Curt inside that big tent talking to those fellows who been griping about the army and the cold and wet outside and how they hated all the same to go back home and pick up where they had left off. No matter how much he might have tried to hold himself in, Curt just couldn't have helped drawing a mighty different picture when he talked about Stehekin. Even when he'd talk about the various disasters that occurred in Stehekin—and that was an awful lot of what happened in Stehekin—he couldn't help telling about them in a way so that you had to laugh. After all, that was how you managed in Stehekin. So most of his buddies wound up with the idea that Stehekin was just about the end of the rainbow, and wished they could go there.

This set Curt to thinking. After all, his folks had a pretty big piece of land and most of it wasn't being used for much of anything. There would be room. Then he thought of the times in the valley when it would have been good if everyone could have got together to do this or that. In fact, this was one of the first ideas Jane and I had when we came to the valley. We had seen some of our stuff thrown off the boat, and unless we came down right away with a truck, it would just sit there to be rained on. So, we asked, why didn't the people of the valley get together and put up a little shed at the dock so things could be out of the weather and you wouldn't have to wait around the dock not knowing whether the barge would get in today or tomorrow. Well, it wasn't a new idea, it turned out; it had been kicking around for a good many years. The answer was that it wouldn't work in Stehekin. Who would build the shed? Where would the lumber come from to build it with? And didn't we know that the boat boys didn't give a damn and wouldn't put anything in a shed even if there were a shed? We retreated in a hurry. But sometime later, when we were sore about the cull stuff the merchants downlake sent us because they figured we wouldn't want to pay the freight for shipping it back, we got the bright idea of the valley's working together to do some bulk ordering and get food and other things wholesale. Well, this wasn't a new idea either and it ran head on into a big set of objections about like the other had.

So Curt put a proposition to his buddies up there on Kiska. Since none of them wanted to go back where they had come from, they would all come up to Stehekin when they got out of the army. They would all work together. There would be a place for everybody to live on the Courtney land and they'd all help each other. But it wouldn't be like the army, no sir, it wouldn't be like the army. There wouldn't be any officers and there wouldn't be any boss, or rather, everybody would be a boss. Nobody would order anybody else around. Everybody would do just what he wanted to do, only of course they would all work together. They'd do the things that needed to be done. Different ones, naturally, had different skills and liked to do different things. So they would be doing different things. But that wouldn't make any difference when it came to dividing up what they had made; it would be share and share alike. Except that maybe there would be times when somebody needed something extra, like paying a doctor or something like that, so he'd get it. And it would be the same way when there was a really cruddy job that had to be done; they'd take turns doing it, or everybody would pitch in and get it done. They'd all eat together and they'd meet to talk and everyone would have his say. And when it was all talked out, there would be one thing to be done and they would all go out and do it. And everyone would work hard because everyone was working for himself at the same time he was working for the others. So there'd never be any reason for one or two of them ordering the others around and telling them what to do.

We, of course, only heard about all this a couple of years later, after we had moved into the valley. It was while Curt was putting in those kitchen cabinets for Jane. He would put his saw down, or whatever it was he was using, and come back to the great plan. It seemed like the least we could do was to listen, and besides, Curt was eloquent. We didn't suggest any difficulties or hint that things might not work out quite the way he was saying they would. We did ask what they would all be doing, however. It was almost an irrelevancy—the answer was, why just lots of things, most anything in fact, clearing land, farming, making furniture, doing things in leather, there wasn't any limit. Why, with that many fellows around you could afford to get some really good equipment, maybe some big stuff.

That was an essential part of the vision: machinery. This was a special love of Curt's, of course, but it wasn't something that he merely tacked on to the plan. Machinery was the key to getting things done, and above all, it was rational. In fact, the plan had the same quality; it was rational. The plan would work for the same reason that machines work—because they have to. And they have to because they're rational. I somehow was reminded of Lenin's definition of communism as soviets plus electricity. Maybe Curt wasn't so simple.

But that was really unfair. Curt had never read anything that you could call radical. And he was a perfectly good American, maybe more so than he knew. So I didn't say anything about Lenin or anybody like him. Instead, we pressed him for other aspects of the plan. He told us a good many details: where the houses would go, what sort of materials he would use (mostly logs and rocks from various places in the valley). And then he would talk about what it would all do for the various individuals who had been there on Kiska. And repeatedly he would try to sum it all up: It would be just like "an old-time community." This phrase kept reappearing, so I asked just what he meant by this. He stumbled and tried hard to explain, but for once words just wouldn't come to him and he couldn't add anything to the statement. It was really our failure for needing to be told what he was seeing.

It was fun talking about it, a bit like a game. We entered into what we thought was the spirit of the thing and pretty soon we were adding suggestions and embellishments to the plan. I don't know when it was, but gradually it began to dawn on us that Curt was in earnest. He did have one of his old army buddies up visiting him when we arrived to live, a pleasant enough fellow who helped Curt put up a little building where he began sleeping as soon as it got closed up. He mostly sat around after that, eating meals with the Courtney's and calling Mamie "Mom," which you could see she didn't like. He seemed to be waiting for something to happen. After a while Curt told us he had written to the other members of his Kiska group and they were all going to come. Pick was merely the first of them.

As the summer approached, another one of the buddies showed up. He sort of hung around waiting too, but the others didn't come. Curt said they were having one kind of trouble or another in getting free, but he was sure they'd turn up. Meanwhile, he was going to get going on starting things so that when everybody was on hand, they'd be set to go. What he did, along with his father and Laurence and the two buddies, was to rig up the old sawmill. First he cut down the brush that had hidden it, and then he started patching. It was a simple rough log-and-plank structure with a slot for the cables to run through when they pull a log through the saw, and a base for the saw and the engine. Stehekin had had a series of little sawmills in the past. The Courtney mill was one; Hugh had set it up a long time before. Frank Lesh had had one and so had Maxwell. None of them ever did much except cut a little rough lumber for a house and a barn or so, and then whenever there had been an attempt to sell lumber, failure had followed. So there weren't many signs of lumbering in the valley except for a few piles of rusted junk and some sawdust mostly hidden by brush.

This time, however, Curt said things were going to be different. The mill was going to be the first undertaking of the buddies. They'd cut lumber for their own houses, and then they'd start selling it. Laurence took the motor out of a truck that had died a few years before and managed to get it set up and running in the mill. Hugh dug out the big circular saw blade, put teeth in it and sharpened them. Curt straightened up the deck and did a lot of other things. The other two fellows helped a bit and stood around. Finally, though, they got the whole thing going. There was an awful racket when they sawed the first couple of logs, and then it all broke down. But that was all right; Curt acted as though he expected this and went back to fixing things.

The real hitch came after it was all set to go. The Forest Service didn't want to sell any logs and seemed to be giving Curt the runaround. He didn't really want very many logs, but what nobody knew yet was that the valley timber had been put by the Forest Service in the "cutting circle" of a mill, a real commercial one, at the foot of the lake. In fact, there were a lot of things we didn't know about the Forest Service. Finally, however, Curt managed to buy a number of trees, and he was set to make a real trial run.

The mill actually ran, and it made boards, good husky ones since Hugh as sawyer—the man who decides what cuts to make on a log—believed in making them extra thick. But the other buddies didn't show up that summer and the mill was pretty shorthanded. Curt had to hire a fellow from downlake to come in and do the logging. He brought a big chainsaw, the first there had ever been in the valley. As I watched him at work, I got a sudden premonition of what he might be able to do if really turned loose. The devastation in the forest just from the few weeks he worked was mighty impressive. But there were breakdowns in the mill and toward the end of the summer, Laurence announced that the old truck engine that had been running the mill had quit for good. So the mill shut down and we decided we were never going to see a real old-time community after all. Curt and the others turned to doing this and that.

We pretty well forgot about the whole thing, and Curt didn't say anything more about his dream, either. Then during the middle of the next winter we had to go downlake and when we got on the boat to come back, there was Curt. He was beaming and it was obvious he was awfully happy about something. He contained himself for a little while and then told us the news: the buddies were coming in the spring as soon as the snow was off. Every last one of them had decided to come this time and they could hardly wait. And Curt had just been downlake to buy a new engine for the mill. And what a fine thing it was, a diesel made just for this sort of job—and a Cat, no less. I don't know which was the greater source of joy, the word from the buddies or the thought of that engine; but, of course, the two were all tied together.

Curt opened up again on the real old-time community; he told us all about the fellows who would be coming in and just what this would do for each one of them and so on. I never saw a happier man, and it was wonderful to listen to. Finally, however, Jane asked him if the buddies were putting up the money for the new engine.

"Well, no," Curt replied. "You see, that's part of it. None of them has anything."

"Then how are you going to buy that engine?" Jane knew pretty well that Curt, like us, didn't have much of anything either.

"Oh, I've got it all arranged. I'm borrowing the money."

"From a *bank*? A bank was willing to loan you money for this?"

"Lord, no. I went to three different banks and I never got so mad in all my life. Why, they wouldn't even listen to me.

They said I didn't have any credit and I didn't have any security and the plan wouldn't work. I've never seen such stupidity. And, man, were they mean!"

"Then, where are you getting the money?"

"Oh, it's all right. I found a man who is in business for himself and he's going to put up the money privately."

The details came spilling out: The loan would be made all right, but at the highest interest rate allowed by the law; in addition, there would be a "bonus" charge of horrendous proportions for making the loan; and Curt would have to get his folks to take a mortgage on their entire place. We gulped as we heard it all. Curt had already signed the contract for the engine and was coming back to get his folks to sign the mortgage. All the gaiety of the trip was gone for us as we got off the boat.

It wasn't any of our business, of course. We had even been prying in asking Curt about his arrangements. We should just stay out of it. But then again, weren't we maybe a little bit responsible? Hadn't we fairly egged Curt on with our suggestions when we thought it was all a fantasy? And anyhow, could we just settle back and watch while Curt lost his shirt and his folks got foreclosed out of their place? We had known from the beginning that Curt was the wildest of optimists. And we knew that his knowledge of downlake and all its sharks and sharpers was as slight as was possible for any adult person in this day and age. We argued it back and forth and the more we did, the sicker we got. Finally we came to rest on the hope that Hugh and Mamie wouldn't sign the mortgage.

We invented an excuse to go down to Courtney's early the next morning. They were still sitting at the kitchen table. We had walked into a family confab, but they were as welcoming as ever to us. And the first thing was that Curt smiled and waved a document at us and said that his folks had just signed and it would go out in the next mail. Hugh and Laurence smiled too, but Mamie looked pretty upset. We had a cup of coffee and went home.

Jane was mad, really mad, by the time we got there. She was mad at Curt, at Hugh and Laurence, she was mad at the company that wanted to sell Curt the Cat, and most of all she was mad at that sharper who wanted to make the loan. And she was mad at all of downlake. I kept rather quiet, but I wasn't happy either. Finally, she announced:

"There's just one thing to do. *We're* going to find the money for that Cat."

I was startled. The thought struck me that if we had not bought our place from Curt, he wouldn't have had the bit of cash for a downpayment on the engine. We were involved, all right. I agreed to Jane's idea.

I think that for a while Curt pictured us as eventual members of the real old-time community. He agreed pretty quickly to Jane's idea, especially after he had to listen to her dressing him and the others down. And the first repayment came quickly, too, in Mamie's look of relief. The signed mortgage went into the kitchen stove and there wasn't a new one and there wasn't a bonus, just a note from Curt. Then he asked if Jane wouldn't do the bookkeeping for the entire operation.

It was insane—the engine, the mill, the scheme, our part in it, the whole thing. At any rate though, we could still hope that it would all evaporate by the time the snow went off.

It didn't. Curt, Laurence and Hugh all went into a flurry of activity, sharpening axes and saws, hunting up peavies and things like that. And just about as soon as it was possible, the barge brought up the diesel. It was big. And yellow. I shuddered at the prospect of its transference to a truck. That very prospect, however, struck right to the core of the engineering instinct of every male in the valley, and all were on hand when the barge came in. Naturally, there was a lot of discussion and there were a lot of different plans. Curt and Laurence let it go on for a while and basked in the glory of it all. Then they quit listening and turned to themselves. They obviously had it all figured out beforehand, you could see that. I half expected Laurence simply to walk over and pick the engine up and set it on the truck. But this was too much, even for Laurence, and anyhow that would have been rather crude. No, the thing was done gently with a few rollers and a chain-hoist. There really should have been cheers for the very elegance of the performance, but by this time Curt and Laurence were panting to get off up the valley and try it out. It took them a while to get it mounted and ready, but the moment came when it was started. Curt stood back and watched while Laurence went through the drill of starting. First the little starter engine came on, and then at just the right moment, Laurence cut in the big engine. It wasn't a loud noise, but it was deep, and the valley reverberated with a throb you felt right down to your boottops. Watching Curt and Laurence, I decided I'd never in my lifetime see such bliss again.

Then the buddies came—they really came. Not all of them nor all at once, of course, but they got to the valley in the space of a week or so. There weren't so many of them by actual count, but it seemed as though our end of the valley had suddenly filled with people. We were glad for the half mile that lay between us and Courtney's and we stayed away for a while, since we thought Curt and the buddies would have a lot of reminiscing to do. So we couldn't tell too well just how things were going.

There were a few signs, however. Maybe the first was when we walked into the Courtney cabin around mealtime. The kitchen was filled with the crew, all around the table, which had been extended with a couple of sawhorses and some kind of makeshift top. Mamie was laying out food, huge quantities of it, which they were all stowing away as though they'd never seen food before. And Curt was sitting at the head of the table in a way we'd never seen before in the household; in fact, there hadn't been a head of the table before. He was joking and kidding with the others, but you could see that it wasn't a matter of chance that he was sitting there.

Our chief source of information was the series of sessions Curt had in the evenings with Jane in her capacity of bookkeeper. He would mainly be up asking her to make out checks for this and that. There were a lot of checks. It was puzzling for a while, since the checks included quite a number to Sears Roebuck and Jane would ask what they were for. Curt would explain that they were for clothes for himself and other members of the family. Curt was surprised that she had asked but more than willing to explain. So she had to deliver another big lecture, this time about separating household from mill accounts. Curt was a little baffled by the idea, but gave in, and she began to get things sorted out.

We'd ask Curt at those sessions how things were going and he was always enthusiastic. Oh, there were problems, sure. Little things, though, things that came up because some of the buddies weren't familiar with this kind of country and had to learn how to do some of the jobs around the mill. And, I gathered, there were a few little problems about living quarters. These were certainly crude, giving protection from rain and not much more. And of course there wasn't any electricity in our whole part of the valley. I had supposed that a bunch of men who had managed to survive up on the Aleutians would be pretty flexible, but apparently some of them were disappointed with how, well, primitive things were in Stehekin. Curt, I gathered, handled that by describing how they were going to change all that.

During the first few weeks we'd hear—or rather feel—the big engine going for a while and we'd know they were sawing. Then it would stop and we'd wonder what had occurred. We happened by a number of times when there were stops. Naturally, I expected that something had gone wrong with the machinery. They seemed to be past this, though. What we saw was that Laurence would put the engine on idle and then everybody would gather up on the deck for a conference. It happened rather often and we supposed that in a new kind of organization such as Curt was planning, there would need to be quite a bit of discussion. The amount that went on, however, was puzzling. And I think I was rather surprised to learn that Curt was having Jane draw up weekly paychecks—even before any lumber had been shipped out. That was the new plan: to ship lumber out for a while to get some cash, and then turn to cutting material for all the houses. But the paychecks went out regularly. It somehow wasn't how I had pictured it when Curt had talked about it in the previous months.

If there were difficulties among the buddies, Curt didn't want to talk about them, and he didn't. The difficulty that we did hear about, however, was the supply of logs. There wasn't any more timber left in the bit that had been bought from the Forest Service earlier, and in order to get the mill started, they were cutting what there was on the Courtney place. And there really wasn't a lot of that; at the rate they were going when they really operated they could get through it fairly soon. Curt was trying to get more from the Forest Service, and it was along then that he learned that the mill down at the foot of the lake was planning to use timber from Stehekin. That mainly meant Forest Service timber, of course, and we gradually got the idea that the government people liked the downlake mill better than they liked Curt. Maybe this shouldn't have been such a surprise. The Forest Service people lived in the same community as the owner of the mill downlake, and the owner just happened to be a big man in politics. And the downlake mill was a real going concern, and had been for a long time. That mill had pretty well cut itself out of timber close to it and easy to get, and so was looking further off. That meant Stehekin, as it turned out. We heard stories from time to time that the downlake mill owner regarded the timber in Stehekin as his timber and was confident of getting it when he was ready.

As most of the Courtney timber came down and got hauled up to the big pile of logs behind the mill, Curt began to get a little desperate. We heard about this from Mamie, who told Jane that Curt and Laurence were wanting to cut the trees in the grove. The grove was something special. It was a cluster of trees—big ones, as trees go in Stehekin— around the old Courtney cabin. They were arrow-straight and almost as tall as trees can get. There weren't a great many of them, but they gave shade to the cabin and the barn, and, well, they were beautiful. They lined up four or five deep in a transparent screen at right angles to the valley axis, and as you came up the road you would see through their line of trunks to the snows of McGregor. Mamie had said no, they couldn't cut the grove. She wiped the corner of one eye with her apron as she told Jane about it. But the boys kept coming back to the subject.

Things seemed to get better in some ways, however. The big engine kept going and never gave a bit of trouble. We heard quite a bit about it from Laurence, who normally wasn't given to a lot of talk. And its stops for conferences got fewer. The lumber was going out regularly now, and there were some checks coming in. They came from the Holden Mine, which was buying everything the mill would cut. It turned out that the mine thought the timbers from Stehekin were the best there were. Not only was the locally-grown timber stronger than that grown anywhere else, but Hugh was laying out cuts that were way more generous than those cut anywhere else. So those Stehekin timbers were absolutely the best thing there was for shoring up all the tunnels and drifts in the mine, which by this time was having a lot of alarming things happen—things like big half-ton pieces of rock popping off the ceilings of solid rock in the tunnels inside the mountain.

By now, Jane had a lot of figures to go on. And she wasn't happy. So it was a big surprise when Curt came up one weekend as the summer was waning. He was grinning from ear to ear.

"We've just had the biggest day yet," he said, and gave the figure for the number of feet sawed.

"I want everybody's salary raised."

"What?" Jane's voice rose above its normal pitch.

"I'm raising everybody's pay."

"Curt, you don't mean it. You can't."

"I mean it. Those fellows have earned it. They're working great. Why, today. . . . "

"You can't do it. You don't have the money."

"Don't have . . . Why, we've been shipping out a bargeload of timber now for . . . how many weeks? And the mine's been paying for it. We've *got* to have the money."

Well, it was true. The money was almost gone. And the sheer running expenses of the mill were bigger than the income. Curt couldn't believe it, and it took a long and horrible evening for Jane to show him it was so. They went over the figures again and again. It wasn't that Curt was slow with figures. He wasn't; in fact, his capacity for figuring in his head was exceptional. He had refused to include expenses for which Jane now had documentary evidence. And over and above all, he had omitted to put any value on the trees they were cutting from the Courtney land. His optimism had been unsinkable right up to the last moment, and it seemed cruel to watch him gradually accept the truth.

So the mill shut down, and the buddies all went downlake. They went so fast that we never even got a chance to say goodbye. There wasn't any farming, or leatherwork or furniture-making or any of the other things that were going to be part of the real old-time community. And there wasn't anybody left to help Curt and Laurence unbolt the big yellow diesel from its foundations and haul it down to the barge. When it went downlake, I'm not even sure that much of anybody was interested in watching it loaded.

It was a while after the cleanup from the whole affair that Curt wandered up to the house and sat down for the evening. He hadn't wanted to talk before, but now he did. The thing he wanted to talk about, however, was not the string of costs that had ended the venture, or any of its business aspects.

"It's funny, you know," he began. "You think you know somebody and you get to be about as good friends as you can be. You tell each other about things you've never talked to anyone about before. And you help each other. Why, man, I thought I knew those fellows. Every one of them. I hiked with them up at that training camp in Colorado and, what I mean, it was cold. And we'd camp out in the snow and you'd swear there wasn't anything any of us wouldn't do for the others. We were all in it together, see? And then up there on Kiska. . . . We talked and we talked until it looked like we had it all figured out. Then, they came up here and it seemed like they were all a different lot of fellows. But they were my buddies, all of them, buddies. I wish I could understand it. Maybe it's that everyone is two people. There's your army self, and there's some other self. I guess I just knew their army selves."

He stayed until late. There weren't any recriminations, either between us or toward the buddies. Just wonder, and maybe a bit of sadness.

9.

Stehekin seemed to attract dreams of utopia—and the dreamers of such dreams. Curt was rather a special case, since he was a native, only of course it was his going downlake to fight in the army that got him going on the real old-time community. The others all definitely came from downlake. Just what it was that did it was a puzzle, but there was a regular flow of them. It wasn't the hippie thing that went on in lots of places, although Stehekin had a hippie commune for a while. (That was much later and was nothing special; it was something continual and persistent.) It was as though there were a peculiarity of the magnetism of the place that set compasses swinging and made one person after another land in the valley and say, "This is the place," and go to work trying to change it.

To hear all the plans that were hatched to make it different, you would have thought that Stehekin was awful—a disgrace to the earth that ought to be erased as fast as possible. This view accounted for at least one group of utopians, the highway people. For them, the fact that Stehekin showed up on the map as simply a dot with no red lines running in or out of it and surrounded by blank space was an insult. It seemed to say to them that here was a spot they couldn't build a road to. They knew that wasn't true, and they were right, of course. But it must have rankled, as they imagined the world thinking that some limit had been found to their abilities. And if this assault to their machismo were not enough, there was the totally unsettling thought that somewhere there might be humans so depraved as not to *want* roads. So Stehekin's challenge to their universal utopia of roads everywhere was understandable in a way. The place was a direct affront and they had to go about changing it.

Curiously, however, they never went about it in a big way. There were a number of reasons. First, it really was true that road building to Stehekin would be difficult. And it would eat up money that would produce a lot more footage of red lines on the map elsewhere. Next, it was hard to think of any excuse to build a road to Stehekin. It wasn't on the route from anywhere to anywhere. It didn't ship much of anything out that anybody wanted. And the people there were so primitive that they didn't even have a native statesman in county government, to say nothing of the state legislature or the United States Congress. There was only that appalling blank space on the map with the letters "Stehekin" printed in the largest type the map makers could contrive to mitigate the great emptiness.

They found an ingenious solution for a while. After running several surveys up to the top of Cascade Pass and discovering what quite a few people had known, beginning with that army officer who looked for a road route to control the Indians back in the nineteenth century—that the way up to it on either side was awfully steep—they decided to pretend. So for quite a number of years the road maps put out by the oil companies showed a pair of dashed lines leading up from Stehekin and out over Cascade Pass labeled, "Cascade Wagon Road." The excuse was that there had once been an entrepreneur who announced a project to build such a road and had actually got a route blazed up the valley a ways before quitting long short of the beginning of the real climb to the pass. Why this was a better precedent than the highway people's own surveys, I don't know. Anyhow, the long abandoned project was no more than a trail where it went. But marking this fictitious road on the map must have made somebody happy, and it was a generally harmless thing to do. That is, it was harmless until some horseback riders decided to try to go this way. There were a number of horses that slipped off one of the ledges it traverses on the east side and were killed on the rocks several hundred feet below, but fortunately they were all being led rather than ridden.

The "Cascade Wagon Road" gave scope, then, and it connected with the roads to everywhere. However, it lacked solidity; the pretense apparently wouldn't allow for more than dashed lines. Once they had decided on this sensible solution, they might as well have made it a solid red line. But they didn't, and had to make up for it some other way. What they hit on was to treat the real road, the one in the valley with two dead-ends, as an official governmentally recognized road. This, of course, could be marked solid with perfectly clear conscience. For a while it was all a county road. Then part of it was made a state highway, State Highway Number 20. They never got any signs up on it, but it got put that way on the maps. Then, when the miners tried to do things up at Horseshoe Basin at the end of the valley, money was pried out of the federal government and it was a Mine-to-Market Road. And then back to a county road again. But all these titles were good enough to justify a good solid blue line. It was only driving over it that might have given anyone doubts.

Curiously, though, they never got around to including the little spur road that lay on our side of the river and ended in our yard; it would have added almost three miles, but I suppose that wasn't worth it. So we did our own road work every year and managed to get over it more or less consistently. But we would have been really stuck over the disappearance of the old swayback bridge if there hadn't been a government-built replacement. This had a title: a Mill-to-Market bridge. It was right close to Art Peterson's sawmill and that, if you except the highway thing—which after all wasn't special to Stehekin—was about the biggest utopia that Stehekin ever saw.

Art Peterson was a visionary. He saw big things and he saw them where other people didn't. He had some of the qualities that led other men before him to imagine a bridge across the Golden Gate, to find a set of tablets giving the basis for a new religion, or to lay out a string of civilized outposts across a heathen land. Only he didn't have the streak of ruthlessness that made people who did those things famous. He wasn't a Stehekinite and he went up and down the lake a lot. So he wouldn't belong in the story except for two things: he had a lot of compassion, and he did things that changed the valley.

He was an orchardist from near the foot of the lake. He had laid out a really big orchard, Delicious apples, like the others down there, and he went through the long period of waiting for the trees to mature and give a cash crop. Then just as he was coming out of this period, times turned bad, and although the trees were doing fine, the market was so poor he would have been better off not to have the trees. Other orchardists were pulling up their trees so they wouldn't have to lay out money for spraying chemicals as the regulations required. Art stuck it out, however, and he showed toughness in doing it. His family backed him up, even though things were thin, and other people began coming to him for help, since he was carrying on. Then there was another turn of the wheel; the war came and times became good. So, when the war was over, good times became great times for the orchardists still in business and there was Art Peterson with a big orchard in full production. A lot of the other orchardists who landed in this situation went wild with their money: big cars, big houses, big boats and so on; they must have been some of the best consumers the economy ever had. But Art had a different set of ideas.

As he did better, an increasing stream of men showed up at the Peterson orchard asking for work and help. Most of them were down and out and they almost always got what they asked for from Art. He knew what it was to have things rough, and he always saw something in a man who was bad enough off to come and ask for help. He would trust anybody. To somebody who wanted work, somebody who looked pretty shabby and seedy maybe, he'd say go down and clear out that irrigation ditch—and keep your own time. Everybody who worked for Art kept his own time and Art always accepted the reckoning. It got so that he was known all over the northwest among the men who drifted from place to place. There was always food, shelter, work when it was wanted—and help—at Art's. So there were always some pretty rough-looking sorts around his place. His neighbors were rather troubled about it and they worried that Art didn't realize he was being cheated right and left by the characters he took on. Maybe he didn't, but more probably he did and didn't care; he was looking beyond the physical needs he was meeting.

It's difficult to tell how or when Art's great idea took shape, but it's certain that the experience of his own hard times and his dealings with all those drifters downlake were the basis of it. And maybe the remarks of his neighbors had something to do with it also. But whether it came before or after he acquired his place in Stehekin, I don't know. Most likely after, since things seemed to grow together for Art without his appearing to think them out. And Stehekin was close to the core of it. His place in Stehekin was, like other private property in the valley, an old homestead that had been proved up on. The place had failed to support the family that had tried to live there, and Art got it at a low price. It had a couple of shacks and an old log barn. Art turned all of these into living quarters with a minimum of patching. And then he began sending up the harder cases among his—well, maybe "clients" is the best word. The attitude of his downlake neighbors was pretty much what the English had when

170

they shipped convicts off to populate Australia.

At Stehekin there were a few doubts about them for a little while. A couple of them were reported to be rather violent, especially when they were drunk. And they managed to be drunk a lot; that was certainly true. They managed it on beer invariably, which was the consequence of the set of laws the righteous legislators of the state of Washington had passed in response to the pleas of the temperance people and the local brewers; hard liquor was awkward to get and expensive, while beer was available in abundance, even in Stehekin. So Hap and Al met the challenge with persistence and diligence in consuming an awful lot of beer. And the stories about violence had some truth, it turned out. Every week or so one or the other of them would show up at the dock with bruises or cuts and generally mussed up, sometimes both of them. But as time went on, it became thoroughly evident that they only fought each other; they never bothered anybody else and they did their fighting in private. So that was their own business and people got to be rather fond of them.

Like a lot of the other folks Art sent up to Stehekin later, they were refugees from the dust bowl of the nineteen thirties. Coming from Oklahoma and Arkansas, they had hit California first, working in the fruit harvests, and then had drifted up to the northwest and its fruit. Their speech was different from anything heard in Stehekin before and everybody used to enjoy listening to them. I think it was Laurence who got to talking with them about the country they had come from. Hap, it turned out, was quite articulate.

The other charge that followed these people uplake was that they probably had a lot of unspecified diseases. So far as evidence was concerned, this was untrue. There was never any epidemic that could be blamed on those people through-out the time they were in Stehekin. Stehekin generally didn't have epidemics, unless you count colds and things like that. And when there was a cold or flu bug that hit the valley, you could always trace it to somebody who had gone downlake and brought it back up. But there was just one case of exotic disease you could trace to those people at Art's place; and this involved a cow. It happened later, when Art began shipping whole families uplake. One of them had a lot of kids and so very sensibly brought a cow along. A month or so after they came, the wife of the family was looking worried down at the dock. Harry asked her if something was the matter.

"Yes," she sighed, "The cow's got hollertail."

"What?"

"The cow's got hollertail."

"What's that?"

"Her tail's got holler."

That stumped Harry and it stumped the rest of us. How did she know? We never found out, and fortunately, the disease didn't spread.

Over the years, a lot of strange people had come into Stehekin and passed through or stayed for a while. But it was interesting that the word "stranger" didn't have a heavy meaning; there wasn't any particular hostility attached to it. Perhaps strangers were more or less expected to be good for a laugh or so; at least nobody in the valley was surprised at anything people from downlake did. And the valley was completely tolerant. However, nothing like the influx of people that Art Peterson sent uplake had ever occurred in the valley before. There had been the buddies of course, but they were not particularly different in any noticeable way and they didn't stay very long. Art's people, however, almost all had their own kind of speech and way of looking at things. There were also quite a few of them and they were in the valley longer. It would have been a strain on most communities, but Stehekin handled it fairly well.

It wasn't altogether clear just what Art planned to do with all those people he sent up, or it never stayed clear for very long. A few of them, like Hap and Al, logged off and on. Then Art sent up a machine he had for making cement bricks. A lot of cement bricks got made, but there was a lot of cement left over after they quit doing that. Art loved doing things with cement; he seemed to feel that when he built, it should be for the ages. But this ran head-on into one of his other ideas—that anybody could do anything. He utterly rejected the notion of specialization, and he had no time for experts, in any field. There was something very attractive about this, since it left him willing to turn any job over to the most unskilled person. This was connected to his deep-down feeling that human beings had to be trusted; if they were trusted, they'd become trustworthy even if they weren't at the beginning. It was a rather nice idea and it seemed to work some of the time. But when he extended the idea to turning somebody without any skill loose on a technical job, it was hard to believe that anybody's confidence got built up; it was depressing to see something built of permanent-looking concrete crack up and fall apart.

Watching from a distance, it was difficult to tell just what was going on at the Peterson place with all that activity. The logging went on sporadically and there would be spurts of things going on with cement, and then suddenly the project seemed to be an electric power system with a big pipeline led down from one of the creeks. Maybe Art had all these things put together in his mind, but maybe also these were just things that he had always wanted to work with, and he turned from one to another as his fancy directed. The electrical plant was a big project, but finally the day came when the water gushed down the pipeline into the cement-brick powerhouse and ran a generator. After some tinkering, it made electricity—a lot of it—and things were lit up in a way never seen in Stehekin before. This was one of the big changes Art's venture wrought in the valley: it made a lot of people unhappy with the lighting systems they had been getting along with contentedly for years. A couple of these were puny little gasoline-driven electric plants, but mostly they were just kerosene lamps.

After the electric plant was going, everybody at Art's turned to building a sawmill. It was to be built of cement and, of course, it was to run on electricity. So things started fitting together, it seemed. The mill was what it was all about and the other things had been mere preliminaries to that. Hap and Al and a couple of the others were busily getting logs to a little pond where the mill was going up, and the place hummed with purpose, so far as we could tell. This obviously would be a different kind of operation than the buddies had tried to run. There began to be moments, however, when it looked like the buddies' operation. Nobody seemed to be in charge and there was a lot of stopping to talk things over. It turned out at this point that Art didn't believe in having a boss around any more than he believed in experts. Somebody would get an idea, let out a yell, and everybody would stop what he was doing to gather and talk it out. Art would show up from time to time, listen for a while, then say

174

this or that should be done, which was about all that got any results. The worst trouble, though, was that since nobody had ever built a sawmill before, some of the results they did get were all wrong. So Art finally gave a little on his prejudice against experts and got Curt and Laurence down to help. But they didn't have any more say than anybody else. It was all run like a Quaker meeting, only noisier, of course.

It was about the time the sawmill was getting ready to go that Art sent up those families with all their kids. For a little while the valley didn't seem to take in what this meant. Everyone was so used to seeing something or another announced and then fizzled away that these families weren't taken seriously as residents. But there they were, expecting to stay. Finally the subject of school came up. Nobody wanted to face it, and it was a while before it came out into the open. Now, Stehekin had a school building, a one-room log structure with a steep shake roof. It had been built in 1926 and had seen Curt, Laurence, Ray, the Buckner girls, and some others who had left the valley through most of the grades, but then the valley ran out of children and it closed. It had been closed for a good many years, in fact. On paper, there was a school district, too. But of course since there was nothing going on in the schoolhouse, everybody had forgotten it.

When the idea of school arose, then, somebody made enquiries and the answer was a big shock. The school district would have to support the school almost completely. The normal help from the state and the county that other communities got couldn't be provided to Stehekin, since a law had been passed to discourage one-room schools like this one and force them to consolidate into big modern establishments. That was what other places had done. But there

175

wasn't any district short of fifty miles for Stehekin district to consolidate with, even supposing that any other place had been willing. The high authorities in the state capitol were appealed to and they sent their sympathy and said that when the law was passed, nobody had thought about Stehekin, so there we were. The children couldn't very well commute downlake and there wasn't anyplace their folks could send them to live there, either.

The next thing was cost. A group of valley residents went down to the school and took a look. It was in bad shape. The roof was sagging and leaking, and the interior had been torn up in successive raids by vengeful Boy Scouts who had camped close by. There were some books in the closet, but somehow it didn't seem likely that books published in 1928 would be right, even where they were still legible after the mice had chewed them. The real shocker, however, was the word that came about a teacher. The teacher would have to have the proper credentials and it wouldn't be possible for somebody from the valley to just go down and start teaching. And the minimum salary for a teacher was larger than the cash income of any regular valley resident.

When this information got around the valley and sank in, the result was what might be called instant politicization. People began going around to each other's houses and talking and arguing for hour after hour. It went on at mailtime at the dock and everywhere. There had to be a special election, first to choose a school board since the old one didn't have exactly proper status, and second to decide on a special property levy. That latter was extra special; in fact, it was huge, since only the biggest allowed by state law would yield enough funds to make a start and pay the teacher's salary. So

Stehekin went from a state of anarchy to a political community in the space of a couple of weeks.

Elections had been held in the valley before, of course, to vote for positions like President, Senator and so on. And based on this, there were Republicans and Democrats. But none of that meant anything in particular, except for those who made wisecracks about the picture of the President that always had to be tacked up in the post office. This was different, and Republicans and Democrats didn't enter into it: it was serious, especially the issue of a special tax.

It was about as bad a situation to start a democracy with as could be imagined. As everybody got to thinking about it, one fact stood out: the tax would fall exclusively on the regular residents of the valley, since they were the ones who owned property, while—with one exception—the only children going to the school would be those of the newcomers. It looked like the class struggle in its purest form: the property owners against the propertyless. In fact, it would be hard to find a meaner statement of the class struggle than the question, "Why should I pay to educate somebody else's kids?" And if you add in that it was also newcomers against established residents, young against old, people of one social background and speech against another, it looked like the making of a lot of trouble. One member of the school board, all of whom were running for proper election, had a good deal to say about it, too. When it was noted that none of the newcomers counted as residents and voters, the election outcome seemed certain, but with a lot of feeling to follow.

Only it didn't turn out that way. The election went off in perfect order with a one hundred percent turnout of the eligible voters in the valley. The special levy won with a better than ninety percent majority. This sort of result is not exactly normal, and maybe it could have raised some questions, but the questions would all have been wrong. The one thing that might have justified a bit of eyebrow raising was what happened in the school board election. Every member was re-elected except the one who had been sounding off. Every ballot except two carried the name of the same write-in opposing candidate, and the valley was able to figure instantly who had cast those two ballots. Chicago's Mayor Daley might have been able to take a lesson in political organization if he had been in Stehekin that day.

So the big issue was settled; the school would open. The school board got busy and organized a big potluck at the school. Everybody turned out and brought tools. Somebody split some new shakes for the roof and the rafters were braced. New steps were cut, the inside was fixed up, and the place was scrubbed from end to end. There was a bonfire of the old schoolbooks that the mice had worked over, and then everybody settled down to the potluck. It was as big a day as there ever was in Stehekin, and not a bachelor in the valley was missing.

Strangely enough, there wasn't any problem about the school teacher. Since it was late in the year, there was only one candidate, but that candidate was right. This was a duly certified grade school teacher, Amy Bell, who brought her husband, a junior college teacher. They both would teach, and when the valley heard about that, everyone felt better about the big salary that was going to be paid out; when divided in two, it didn't sound so bad, even though it still hurt the budget. But the best thing about this arrangement was that it was a faculty that had a bit of background for Stehekin; they had both come from nearby valleys.

All told, it made a fairly unusual school. Amy was the teacher officially hired the first year, and Lloyd was unofficial helper. For the second year, Lloyd got the right kind of license and he was hired as the teacher, while Amy was unofficial helper. It gave a four-to-one student-faculty ratio, and this was pretty good by any comparison. The parents and some of the other people in the valley had been worried about the kids getting enough discipline, but this didn't seem to be a problem. When things got too rambunctious, Lloyd simply took down his fishpole and moved the seventh grade arithmetic class, or whatever he was teaching at the moment, outside a hundred feet to the bank of Rainbow Creek and carried on. Of course the problems got phrased in things like, if you catch three fish an hour, how many would you catch in ten and a half hours? But this, after all, was practical—you might say relevant—learning. The other consequence was that the school wound up with a total of only two rules: 1) It is forbidden to fall into Rainbow Creek, and 2) It is forbidden to get bitten by a rattlesnake.

Watching that school raised some real questions about the other schools, the ones that public policy said were the only right kind. In the one room, all the kids were thrown together and sorting out the grades wasn't very clear. Some of the students would be given books to read or other things to do while others were being taught something else by one of the teachers. Naturally, this sometimes meant that those studying would be listening to what was going on with the others. Generally, it seemed to make for one of two things. Either the class reciting or being taught would be ahead of those supposed to be studying and these would surreptitiously try to catch on so that they could pull a surprise by knowing what they hadn't come to officially yet, or the class going on would be at a lower level and the older students would start helping the younger. Sometimes Lloyd and Amy would shut these things off, but gradually they came to take advantage of them. Certainly the kids showed enthusiasm for school, which is, after all, one of the tests that ought to be applied.

The more interesting consequence of throwing all grades into the same room was that the differences in ages didn't seem so important as might have been assumed. They all knew each other well and if there were to be a ball game at recess, for example, the teams would have to include a mixture of ages and sizes. In a way it reflected what happened in the valley generally; the differences between ages turned out to be much less important than the differences between individuals. People weren't just a cluster of categories. But the differences between individuals did get recognized in the school, just as in the valley generally, and this made for a situation different from that found in the proper modern schools. The principal effect was that it made much more for cooperation than for competition. But, of course, this meant it was probably bad training for life downlake. All the same, the sort of toleration for human difference that showed up in the school seemed rather desirable. So the great school crisis passed and it wasn't bad after all, and the school turned out to reflect Stehekin much more than downlake.

If the starting of the school was the most obvious impact of Art Peterson's ventures, there were others that were just as important and maybe more so. They only became apparent later, and they probably had other causes as well. They tended in fact to feed each other and to merge, so that it became difficult to see where one left off and the others began, even to tell which was cause and which was effect. One of them, however, came fairly early: the issue of electricity. Not only did those newcomers get a school for themselves; they got electricity for the places they lived in. And as Art himself pointed out, his plant turned out more power than he could use. The thought that other people in the valley could also have electricity ate its way like an acid into the consciousness of quite a few households. The nearby region downlake had just been through a big struggle by a Public Utility District to take over the plant and lines of a private electric utility, and one of the big arguments was that the public body wouldn't merely think of profits, but would see that the rural areas got electrified. So somebody in Stehekin started badgering the P.U.D. with the argument that Stehekin was as rural as it was possible to be and that the P.U.D. ought to prove up on the propaganda that had been made for it. The P.U.D. replied that this was different and they hadn't meant a place like *Stehekin.*

Naturally, this response made a lot of the valley people mad, and they joined up with those who were only panting for electricity and had suddenly discovered that they had eye trouble from reading by kerosene lamps, and a campaign got going. There were some things that the P.U.D. might have said, such as that the people in Stehekin had got along fine without electricity and a good many other things so why couldn't they just continue, but they didn't. The fact was that the P.U.D. people were cornered; they really believed it was impossible to live without electricity and that everybody had to have it. So some engineers came uplake and looked around. They came up with a number of schemes, such as running a cable up the lake along the shore or even below the surface. The cost figures were horrendous and the P.U.D. tried to wiggle off the hook again. They were caught, however, and finally agreed to run Art's plant and string wires around the valley.

Not everybody signed up for electricity, but most people did. Once the P.U.D. had given in and other people had the stuff, it was hard to refuse to go along. Besides, it was pointed out during the signup campaign that just to take it for lighting would save money over buying and hauling kerosene. But that's not where it stopped. People began buying refrigerators and toasters. Then there were vacuum cleaners and electric ranges. The list was enormous, and before long Stehekin was engaged in the biggest buying spree there had ever been. A number of people bought a couple of electric heaters, and then somebody decided to do all his heating with electricity. The cost of electricity sounded low, since it was just a matter of wiring; water would be coming down the big pipe to the generator continually anyhow and rates weren't high, so why not? Other people decided to hook their water systems up with electricity so they wouldn't have to pump by hand or mend intakes and so on.

Of course, in no time at all the Peterson plant broke down and the engineers were back. They came in groups and they came frequently; they were probably the only people in the P.U.D. who liked the idea of having taken on Stehekin, since they came up most often in fishing season. After some trials and failures with the Peterson plant, they said there would have to be a new plant; the old one was really not big enough.

The next link in the chain of consequences was a big one.

Everyone needed a lot more money. Buying some of those appliances and wiring and fixtures had been easy enough to start through installments. There had always been some buying on credit in Stehekin, but things were on a different scale now. And the cost of the electricity turned out to be considerably higher than it had looked, especially by those who decided to heat with it. No study was ever made, but it is fair to guess that the increase of consumer debt in Stehekin was enormous. This was when some of those families that had come uplake to escape their problems and stay forever decided to move out. Others, including some of the long-standing residents, looked for ways to get more money.

The change was more gradual than this sounds and hardly anybody was aware of how far it had gone, unless it was Curt. He and Laurence didn't stay with the Peterson sawmill for very long, and seemed to find the whole thing ridiculous. Maybe the similarities with the buddies' venture were too obvious, but for whatever reason, Curt stopped talking about a real old-time community. He turned to doing various things. One of them was building houses. Some of them were for downlakers who had come up and bought bits of land in the valley—vacation homes, they were called. Then he divided up a little acreage he had of his own and built similar houses on the lots. Although he started by doing the work himself, pretty soon he was hiring men who came up from downlake to do the work. There were not a lot of these houses, since the demand was less than heavy.

All of these things, however, were fairly small changes. To look at any one at the time would have been to dismiss it as hardly worth attention. It was only when they were added up that they might have seemed significant. And anyhow, the real transformation of the valley economy came over the road. This was a curious thing, for the road still didn't go anywhere and it still had the dead-ends it had always had. As the Peterson mill began to falter and as things didn't seem to move along there, Curt began to worry. Although he had never expected big things from that mill, he didn't like the thought of so many people moving out of the valley. The scheme he put together in response was probably one of the most ingenious and effective pieces of economic planning since the days of Germany's Hjalmar Schacht.

Although Curt never articulated it in so many words, this is how it went: In order to support the new standard of living, the valley needed more people. (Or just possibly Curt figured the other way around; he was gregarious.) In order to have more people, there had to be jobs. The most consistent source of potential jobs was the road. But these jobs would be seasonal unless the road were kept open the year round by clearing snow. In order to provide a need to keep the road open, the school had to be kept going; otherwise the county, which now had the entire road in its charge, would ignore the going-nowhere road in Stehekin.

It was wonderfully neat and it dovetailed precisely with the other things that Curt was doing, especially the houses he was building and the old beat-up cars he brought uplake to rent out to tourists a bit later. So he lobbied the county government persistently for more road maintenance, and a number of other valley people lined up behind him. Since he was so knowing about the road and all its problems, the county made him their local highway supervisor and told him to go to it. He wasn't on salary and got paid only for the time he actually put in on the road, which wasn't a great deal. The county apparently thought that by not sending an engineer up and down the lake, they had found a way to get by in Stehekin without its costing anything. They got disillusioned later.

So Curt spent quite a bit of time persuading some of those people Art had sent uplake not to move out. And when he failed, he worked hard to get others to move uplake, always families with a number of kids. There was always the specter that the number of children of school age in the valley would fall below the minimum necessary to keep the school open. Ultimately, Ray's family would provide the needed numbers, but as yet his boys were too young. So there was a more or less steady stream of families coming into the valley, staying for a while and then moving out. They kept the school open and the road hummed with activity the year round, since Curt always promised the new families work on it.

The road changed, too. The little strip of green between the wheel tracks was the first thing to go. Then in one place after another, the road got wider. Some trees that had stuck out into it got pushed down, and little bends were straightened out. It seemed as if there was always somebody digging rocks out of the tracks, but there were always more; and anyhow, the holes that were left where the rocks had been removed made bumps that were just as bad as the humps had made. But while it would be hard to say that the road was improved, the Gross Valley Product had certainly gone up.

There were other changes in the valley, too. It would be difficult to tabulate them in any orderly way, but those who had known Stehekin before felt them in a multitude of ways. In the first place, there were people in the valley at any moment who couldn't quite be placed. Then there was the feeling that came when a car would go by without stopping to pick up somebody walking. This didn't happen often, but it did happen. There were fewer valley get-togethers and pot-lucks, and those that were held were awkward in ways hard to define. But I suppose the thing that dramatized the change more than any other was that Laurence moved downlake. For good. He got married to the society editor of the paper of a nearby town, the one that's advertised in big letters at the top of the front page as "The Apple Capitol of the World and the Buckle of the Power Belt of the Great Pacific Northwest." It was a big shock.

The Peterson mill didn't do much after the first big flurry. The crew got involved with a number of other things for a while—getting a planer set up and so on. But then some of them went back downlake, and even Hap and Al drifted off. It looked as though something was wrong with the mill, especially after the roof caved in under the weight of the snow one winter and wasn't fixed. This wasn't the story, however. It turned out that the sawmill had never been what the Peterson thing was all about. No, Art finally let us in on what he was doing. He was going to build a big resort, a beautiful one. It would have a lodge and cabins and other things to go with them. But the main thing was a golf course. All the logging had been done along the fairways he had laid out for the course which he showed us one day. The logs that had been cut to clear the fairways would be sawed up in the mill for lumber for the lodge and cabins, just as the cement blocks had been made to build the mill and the powerhouse. It all fit together, and one thing had merely been preliminary to another.

But the golf course was really what it was all about in the

end. The crew took out stumps and then ploughed the fairways. And Art planted grass, beautiful grass. He seemed to forget about the mill, the electric plant, and the resort. He concentrated on the grass, which he watered himself, going from one fairway to the next turning on the sprinklers. He never put in any greens, though. The reason, we were told, was that to do so would make the place taxable as a golf course and Art wasn't ready for that yet. He didn't play golf himself, but for the whole time he was around, Art saw to it that the fairways were mowed and he carried out the watering like a religious ceremonial. The last thing I saw of him, he was walking along one of those emerald fairways with the long iron key he used to turn on the sprinklers, looking up at McGregor. I don't think he ever realized what he had triggered in the valley.

10.

Looking back
on those later years,
it was as though an invisible and poisonous
cloud had crept up the twisting canyon of Lake
Chelan. A considerable time passed before we
were conscious of it. There were portents, of
course, and we should have paid them more attention. But their meaning was as obscure as the
clicking of a geiger counter to the inhabitants of
a Pacific atoll.

The passage of time continued to be measured
by the seasons—the first red flare of vine maple,
the first valley snow, and the rise and fall of
waters. It was measured, too, in the span of hu-

man life. Olive Buckner, Mamie and Hugh Courtney, Jack Blankenship, the Leshes, the Wilsons, Dad Imus, Daisy, one by one lived out their lives and were gone from the valley. They went with the memories of older things, and had no need to know the meaning of signs beginning to appear.

The sense of space as it had been from the beginning persisted. Less vivid, perhaps, and with insensibly changing colors, but still it seemed the same. But this was already an after-image. Unseen from Stehekin, the boundaries had shortened and the area contracted. Like a plain before a flow of lava, the earth outside came under a seared and deathly sameness. The flow reached to the edge of the mountains and entered the outer valleys, but it remained out of sight from inside the mountain world. As before, that world seemed to go on and on. To reach the crest of any of the ridges was as hard and long a pull as before. And from any of the heights above Stehekin, the peaks went on in a succession that vanished in a distant haze which could have been taken as a rendition of infinity itself. In such an expanse it was hard to believe there could be an end to either space or time.

The first of the signs was not only open, but blatant. But it was not to be taken seriously, and we missed the meaning, which indeed was slightly beneath the surface. The ridiculous fact was that an attempt was going to be made to develop Horseshoe Basin. Indeed, there would be two attempts, since two groups were making independent and separate efforts with different claims. Horseshoe Basin is an impressive cirque near the head of the valley. The horseshoe figure is apt, except that it suggests nothing of the two big peaks looking down on the basin. Both rise in cliffs and are connected by a spine of rock that has its own expressive name, The Ripsaw. Below the crags, several sloping shelves carry deep snow, and one of them has a steep little glacier. The snow and the glacier feed a group of waterfalls whose number varies from nineteen to twenty-five. It is grand, spectacular, and not a little forbidding, especially in bad weather when the wind pours over the cliffs like the waterfalls. In two minutes a cloud can close off the sky over the basin; the dark walls press in toward each other, and even the waterfalls seem menacing.

The presence of minerals at Horseshoe Basin has been known since the last quarter of the nineteenth century. A long band of rust stretches across two thirds the length of the cliffs, evidence of mineralization to the most amateur prospectors. And not a few gunny sacks of heavy and glittering rocks have been carried out for display to gullible investors. Probably most of the various stock promotions focused on the rocks of Horseshoe Basin were made in good faith, if that is the right term, for the promoters themselves seemed invariably to have faith in abundance. It was certainly little more than that, since the facts of the basin were highly adverse. The bits of flashy minerals appeared only in small discontinuous pockets, since the rocks of the area had been severely faulted and shifted by the rise of the range. The various tunnels and drifts which were driven in the rock quickly lost the small streaks of metal they started with. The costs of operation were high, and accompanied by real elements of danger. The tools and primitive machines which were brought in came mostly by pack animals, and even the timber for shoring up the broken rock of the tunnels was hard to get. Substantial operation was possible for only a short time each year, five months at most. And had some real strike been made, there would have been a requirement of massive investment to force a route out to any smelter.

Even such facts as these, however, lacked the power to penetrate the determination of one group after another bent on creating that "second Butte," which had been proclaimed in Chelan early in the century. This was a zeal unalloyed by any of the love for the hills that sent individuals like Jack Blankenship off to the remoter spots to do "assessment work" on not-quite-believed-in claims. And yet, Horseshoe Basin was a local legend. During the years of greatest excitement, just after the turn of the century, the upper valley held more people than it ever has since. During one winter, the rumor of a strike sent a hundred panting would-be prospectors far up the valley to the last spot where a safe and semicomfortable camp could be made. A "hotel" was even built for their accommodation. It could have been little more than an array of shacks; no remains of the establishment have been visible for many decades. And it can hardly have been a harmonious camp, since the only reason for the presence of any of its clientele was mutual suspicion that one of them would get a successful start before the others. In the meantime, their principal occupation would have been watching for the first half-safe moment to proceed into the avalanche-swept upper valley.

The more tantalizing story was of a dozen "Russians" who actually spent one winter in the basin itself. They were not in the floor of the cirque, but on the sloping shelf above it that is euphemistically called the "Upper Basin." Certainly, they were safer there, since the avalanches starting at the base of the Ripsaw swept over the tunnel they lived in and piled up below in the floor of the basin. Even so, the story goes, twenty lengths of stovepipe were necessary to bring air into their tunnel. Who were these Russians and how were they induced to bury themselves in a spot worse than any Czarist Siberia? The story ends without an answer. And there is the further item that a Miss George lived up in the basin and was the one who snowshoed down to the lake for the mail, twenty-three miles each way. Was this true? Could it have been? The upper valley for its last five miles is appallingly dangerous in winter from the avalanches on either side that meet and cross each others' tracks. How did she survive? How long did she take to cover that distance and return? How often did she try it? And why? Again, unanswered questions. But we knew Miss George slightly; she was still living in the valley when we first arrived, one of those two sisters for whom Curt and Laurence always cut winter wood. Though tempted to ask for her story, we never did; there was a mute understanding in the valley that her privacy was to be respected.

After that period, there were recurrent efforts to open the "mines" in Horseshoe Basin. If the tunnels were carried just a bit further... the dream seemed invincible. And each time money ran out. So Stehekin was not inclined to take the announcement of still another attempt very seriously. But early one spring the barge began to come uplake rather frequently. It brought quantities of material: ore cars, mining track, drill steel, and so on. All of it was used and heavily rusted, a familiar sign to the followers of the basin; these were shoestring operations. Absurd though they might be in relation to the difficulties, however, they were yet capable of making a series of monumental messes—at the dock, at the end of the road and along the way. What happened about the road was more startling, though. Closed as usual toward the upper valley by flood, a new route was to be created to avoid the worst danger from the river, and the road was to be actually extended into the basin. The costs would be enormous and the skeptics laughed at the first word of the idea. But the laugh was the other way. The new road would be built—all the way into the basin—and it would be paid for by the federal government. This was the secret weapon of the new ventures; a new law provided money for roads such as this, and it could be commanded by outfits like those now preparing to exploit the upper valley. If there was ever any doubt what values the nation was prepared to authenticate, here was incontestable evidence, and the sign we should have seen.

For several years, the upper valley was filled with the racket of machinery and dynamite. The road opened to a spot just below the basin, and a way was scraped and clawed to the main adit inside the basin. The whole thing was a brutal undertaking, and the wreckage was impressive. The last two miles were bone-loosening to travel, but several vehicles consistently traversed them. The miners laid out a cable that was to be strung aerial fashion from the upper basin all the way to the floor of the valley. They deepened several of the tunnels and built two buildings of corrugated iron in the floor of the valley, down a bit from a direct line leading into the basin. These buildings, quarters for the crews at work above, were quickly surrounded by mounds of arriving equipment and debris from the operations. What had once been a wild and awing spot was transformed, seemingly overnight. We had grossly underestimated the capabilities of industry, even small industry.

We should have seen it as a major catastrophe. The

curious fact, however, is that we did not. Certainly it was unsettling to see what devastating change could take place, but there were reasons for ignoring it. The first was that the mine and the upper road provided occasional work for some of the neighbors, notably Curt and Laurence. It was work at good pay, moreover. This was the persistent and insidious thought that time and again paralyzed rational evaluation of what should have been seen as a matter of fundamental choice: some friend, some human being will gain some end he desires; job, profit, or whatever. Since this is what he and others like him want, it must be accepted as good, whatever private doubts one may have. And from this, there is only a single step to rationalization of the paralysis of response by reference to the tattered notion of progress.

The other reason for avoiding thought about Horseshoe Basin was the valley's disbelief in the miners' prospects. This was dramatically justified in the spring after the metal sheds were built. Winter came early in the basin and the upper valley. Several near misses by small avalanches finally persuaded the miners to shut down for the season, and they left the country. The winter was one of moderately heavy snow that was late in leaving the valley. The next June, one of the miners came uplake and explored the road to where snow still closed it, then chartered a small plane to look over the route in order to estimate when operations might begin for the new season. He returned to Stehekin with a curious story: he had been unable to see either the mining buildings or anything else that was familiar below the basin. The weather had not been good, of course, and he had not been able to get down very low into the valley, but he was obviously puzzled. He checked with several valley people about landmarks, as though he thought he might have lost his way. He shortly left to go up the valley by foot.

He came back a shaken man. The buildings had indeed disappeared, as had everything else of human make. An avalanche of epic proportions had swept down from the highest point of the upper basin just below The Ripsaw, poured over the cliffs into the main basin and then down into the valley. It had then made a right angle turn and flowed down the valley for a quarter mile, neatly bypassing the ridge that was presumed to be protection for the camp. When we saw it in July, the fan was seventy-five feet of compacted snow and ice on top of the spot where the camp had been. Tree trunks eighteen inches in diameter had been snapped off and were imbedded in the debris. The inch and a half cable laid out for the tramway was scattered in a dozen pieces. Much of the avalanche fan was still there a year later. The Horseshoe Basin mines were finished for good. As if for emphasis, more than a mile of the new road was erased in a flash flood in the fall of the same year. The torrent left its old bed and took the course of the road; a boulder-strewn gulch with ten-foot vertical sides was the only indication where the road had been.

So to the other reasons for complacency, there now was added the belief that the country was able to take care of itself. So thoroughly had the natural events of the upper valley done their work that not only was it difficult to trace the onetime route and find the exact campsite, it was exceedingly difficult to walk up the valley. As for the relocation of the road lower down, it was abandoned and shortly became so overgrown that it, too, was hard to find. The vindication of valley wisdom could hardly have been more complete.

Or more false.

In all the petty confrontations between Stehekin and downlake, it had seemed that here were two worlds separated by the outer ranges of the Cascade uplift and only tenuously connected by the canyon of Lake Chelan. The contrast between the two outlooks was at times as sharp as if they had been two distinct cultures. The distance between them, however, was one of time. The cultures were the same. Had the lake's canyon been less twisting, it might have been possible to imagine it as a window for the nation to look upon its own past. So looking, it might have seen itself in the last moment before the crossing of a shadow line. The issue before human life in Stehekin, the one transcending all others, was the same as that prevailing downlake; but just as there, it was hidden by its very transparency. It was recognition of the terms of the covenant by which human existence could go on without destruction of the other things of the earth.

In the history of Stehekin—or America—it would be hard to say that such a covenant had ever been recognized. Instead, there was the myth of a virgin land: a place—a continent—without history, waiting for the arrival of its master to enter into its possession. The nearly incredible fact is that even before the beginning of the republic, an antithesis between man and nature had been established as the matrix for subsequent events. Two centuries were enough to complete the conquest of a continent; far less was needed for a valley overlooked through the accidents of time. The zone of what could be tolerated by that nature which had been declared the enemy was large, and its capacities for recovery from damage were often greater than might have been assumed, as the big avalanche in Horseshoe Basin showed. But the fact that no limits had been reached was fragile evidence for the belief that no limits existed.

The ventures of the people of the valley seemed little different in kind from those that had long been underway downlake. They were, however, vastly different in scale. It would be good to believe that within the valley, a sense of limits might have developed earlier than downlake, because the values of the valley people had not yet become the desiccated things of downlake. In truth, however, the process of withering had begun, and there was little resistance when the real assault from downlake began.

It began in an atmosphere of stealth. There was a rumor, only that, of the announcement of a sale of timber in the Stehekin Valley. According to the story, bids had been asked by the United States Forest Service for a block of timber somewhere in the valley, and this was to be the first of a series of sales. What was the basis of the story? Somebody—Ray, perhaps—had seen a dittoed sheet of the announcement. Yes, Ray had seen something like that, but he couldn't find it. The thought of a sale by the government was something staggering to contemplate. Most of the land—all save a few original homesteads, in fact—was public. Originally part of the old public domain, it had passed into a forest reserve and then been handed over to the U.S. Forest Service as part of a national forest. Once a policy of systematic logging was begun in the area, there would be no point at which it could be expected to stop, other than the availability of trees and the limits imposed by cost. Economic feasibility was plainly indicated by the announcement, if announcement there was. The other thought which rushed to the surface was that since the buddies' mill was now a thing of the past and the Peterson mill plainly moribund, the sale would be for the benefit of the mill at the foot of the lake. The idea of a monopolistic standing for this mill had been implicit in the policy of a "cutting circle," which had already been declared.

It was one of those moments that come occasionally in every lifetime; instants not of revelation but of realization, when a series of long-known facts suddenly arrange themselves in a pattern of certainty which a moment before would have been unbelievable. In a matter of seconds, the seclusion and the uniqueness of Stehekin vanished as though it had been a mirage. The valley had already had demonstrations of chainsaws and large bulldozers. The downlake mill-owner had made no secret of his intentions. And the Forest Service had proclaimed in the word of its chief that it was "no longer a custodial agency."

The shock of realization was followed by a sense of helplessness, the same sense that had long been the daily companion of life downlake. It was something new in Stehekin. True, there had always been awareness of natural difficulties: cold, a stony earth, heavy snow, and all the rest. And the prospect of disasters from flood and fire and avalanche had always been vivid. These, however, were comprehensible. They were conditions of life that could be planned for, and against whose occurrence prudence was a protection. The simple resources of individual effort, moreover, had meaning in their face. Wood could be cut, the soil improved and the snow traversed. Given only the conditions of humility and a sense of inclusion among the things of nature, there was the paradox that human individuals could share in the direction of their own destinies. And even though conditions were more stringent in Stehekin than downlake, the rewards were vastly greater.

The assault from downlake, then, was something different in kind. Always threatened and frequently announced, until now it had failed to materialize. And the valley was unequipped to deal with it. Indeed, the special valley traits that had served so well in coping with the adversities of normal life became handicaps. The recognition that disaster was possible and the tolerance for the views and projects of others, which in the past had produced cooperation without organization, were not irrelevant; they made for resignation and acceptance.

The important part of the rest of the story took place downlake. It started with inquiry at the headquarters of the national forest, which might as well have been Kafka's Castle. The Supervisor was away; what was the inquiry about? To discover whether the rumors in Stehekin were correct. Mmnn, well I don't know anything about that. Maybe Mr. Blank could help. Mr. Blank was in but busy, very busy, as his manner proclaimed when the inquirers were in time admitted. A sale of timber in Stehekin? He had heard... but, no, he didn't know about it. Maybe Mr. Faceless would know. Mr. Faceless joined the impromptu conference. Stehekin? The Supervisor would be the one to see. But the Supervisor was away. Didn't anybody else know such things? Mmnn... well, yes, there had been some thought of selling timber in Stehekin a while back, but, well no, there weren't any present plans... the Supervisor....

It had a dreamlike quality. Nothing was definite, nothing was sharp or clear. Figures were moving about behind some kind of gauze screen, but who they were or what they were doing, or even if they were anything more than shadows, was impossible to tell. And yet, there was a pervading feeling of menace, of something hard and evil impending. But if the Supervisor existed, perhaps he would respond to a piece of paper. A letter was written and carefully addressed to him. Days went by in Stehekin as we waited for a reply. Ray, meanwhile, had cudgeled his memory and become certain he had seen the announcement; he described its appearance, the spacing of the text and the gist of what it had said. The date of the sale was just three weeks away. Those of us who were not yet resigned—and there were a few—haunted the post office each day for some response from the Supervisor, but it did not come. Then, the day before the date of the sale as Ray remembered it, a Forest Service trail crew foreman appeared at the dock and dropped a single sentence out of the corner of his mouth to one of his valley friends: the sale had been postponed. The word raced around the valley. But it was a week later before the letter came from the Supervisor. Reduced in length, it said flatly that the rumors had been wrong; the Forest Service had not planned any sale in Stehekin and the concern had been entirely needless. But of course there might be a time in the future when a sale might be necessary.

It was astonishing and, after the first moment of relief, as weird as what had gone before. As time went by, it became clear that it had been quite real—round one, in fact—and to our complete amazement, the outcome had been a draw. Whatever satisfaction we derived from this was more than counterbalanced by the intimation of the subterranean char-

acter of the thing that was coiled downlake. Its real importance was that inadvertently, we had been given a warning, a
warning which we had abundant reason to heed in the years
that followed.

That the downlake mill owner should covet the timber
growing in Stehekin was comprehensible. His mill had approached the end of its supply of more accessible logs; what
stood in Stehekin was simply next on the list. And it was unthinkable to him that there should be resistance, even objec-
tion. Small though this enterprise was in the industry or the
state, it was the largest industry in the locality. By a hallowed
tradition, locally made decisions were best; and the processes
of decision were structured in terms of the mill's locality. The
purpose of the mill was to make lumber, and its test of ef-
ficiency was financial success. By experience, the owner of
the mill had every reason to believe the demands of the mill
would be met, and by reflection, he may even have regarded
its operation as a calling.

The process would not have gone as far as it did in the
Forest Service, however, if it had not been supported by a
very particular set of beliefs. So far as Gifford Pinchot, the
first chief of the Forest Service, was concerned, these were all
summed up in a phrase he had picked up in his education
and which he came to regard as his own invention, "The
greatest good of the greatest number in the long run." The
destruction of the forests was evil because it benefitted only a
few and because it was wasteful. But the "good" that the
forests offered was what the greatest number of individuals
wanted from it, and the best test of this was the market.
What could be tested on the market, of course, was what

could be bought and sold, and in the case of the National Forests this was sawlogs. The logic was very simple: the purpose of the National Forests was to produce lumber; the area around Stehekin was National Forest; the purpose of the Stehekin area was to produce lumber. It was neat and comprehensible to a big bureaucracy. In time it received a gloss with the slogan, "multiple use," but this only meant that competing "uses" were to be judged by the administrators, who would decide as they thought best.

The doctrine was in various ways a hideous parody of the democratic creed the nation professed, and it produced appalling results. In the name of individual choice, it asserted the power of bureaucrats; in the name of conservation, it presided over the systematic clear-cutting of forests; in the name of multiple use, it recognized but a single kind of good: the marketable.

In the course of time, the forest supervisor appeared in Stehekin. He was real after all, so we sat outdoors together beneath a sky still glowing in the dusk of a northern summer. He was big, jovial and hearty, and he wanted to talk to the members of the little group that had been writing letters to friends and acquaintances. He wanted to explain a few things, even to hear what other people had to say. It was impossible to dislike the man, for he wanted to be friendly. He began with an expression of tolerance for a different point of view. He, too, loved to get into the great out-of-doors, and he regretted every day he had to spend with papers in an office. It was good for people to be in the mountains. . . . Minute by minute he became more the great outdoorsman and his chest expanded visibly with deep pulls of the pure mountain air. He *understood*.

Well-rehearsed and off-key as it was, the speech still had a note of sincerity. In some remote corner of his being, a chord was vibrating in sympathy to something—a memory of himself, perhaps, as he had been long years before. But the period ended; his face became serious and his voice grew cold. The trees of the valley would be cut. Left standing, they would die and topple over with no good to anyone and this would be waste, sheer waste. And the same was true for the timber of the Agnes and . . . he named every other valley and area of the region where trees grew that could be reached. One by one, all would be sold and harvested for the good of mankind. To object would be sentimental, selfish and futile. The coming sales were necessary, and they would take place.

There was nothing, after all, that could be said to him that he could hear. He had said what he had come to say and what he believed—and what was national policy. He sat in silence for a while, then took up his hat and, jovial once more, remarked on the splendor of the evening and left.

* * *

In a way this was the end. But of course there are no ends in reality, just as there are no beginnings. Things did not develop as it seemed they must that night of the supervisor's call at Stehekin. The future of Stehekin and of the entire North Cascades of which it was a part became a concern to numbers of people across the nation. Just as the supervisor had said, this was a national matter. The timber sales were rumored again, but there were increasingly loud protests from astonishing places: New York, Massachusetts, Wisconsin, California. Some of them were from travelers who had seen the region and hoped to return. Others were from people who had never seen it and doubted they ever would, but who simply considered it good there should be such a place left unblemished. The sales were again denied—and postponed.

It is rare for any people to reflect upon its own values or question in a serious way the course it has travelled. Yet this has happened in the United States in the second half of the twentieth century. It came in response to a kind of radicalism that denied essential parts of the human heritage; an extremism that denied recognition to any limits to human endeavor save those imposed by technology. It was a radicalism that perceived man as separate, apart, and above the natural firmament in a wholly Ptolemaic vision. And, embarked on a war of total conquest in the name of human well being, it produced a condition in which humans were reduced to objects of administration and induced to deny essential parts of their own humanity. It produced its own reaction.

The catalyst was direct experience of the degradation that was taking place. It was immediate, direct and specific. Where before, the changes were so gradual that it was possible to be ignorant of what had been lost—and so not to miss it—the pace now quickened so that it was visible, like the racing movement of a clock whose regulator has failed. In one place after another—places of special quality that spoke of timeless things—the assault came close. And spontaneously, it aroused an indignation of deep intensity. At first there were only a few prepared to protest or give even a token of resistance, but each time a voice was raised, it developed there were others who shared the sense of outrage. And so the myth of a monolithic national commitment to total conquest was cracked.

Stehekin was one of those places where the catalyst took effect. As a sop to the resistance, the Forest Service announced a plan for a wilderness area that would have left untouched only an area incapable of growing trees worth cutting. The downlake mill-owner moved into the valley and began to log a few pieces of private property while he waited impatiently for the Forest Service to solve its public relations problem. These steps, however, only resulted in a further coalescence of opposition. What this won seemed for years to be no more than delay, but this was vital; for year by year the opposition became more organized and more effective. So ultimately the issue reached Congress, and after thirteen years of struggle, some limits to the destruction were made national policy. It declared two wilderness areas of substantial size, a national park, and several other areas—one including Stehekin, in which protection against destruction was to be enforced.

The legislation was not perfect, and neither was the concept it embodied. The areas "created" were proclaimed to have purposes—human purposes—and so in one sense, the ill was as deep as ever. It might have been better to assert that these were sacred places. Useful though such a metaphor might have been, however, it would still have been false, for the remainder of the earth would have lacked equal recognition. One fact nevertheless stood out: some limits had been acknowledged. A highway would not enter the valley, and the Stehekin road would continue its meander to nowhere. And the threat of logging was ended.

The human community of Stehekin changed. Its older members died and some of the others moved out, Curt and Beryl among them. I don't think Curt made another attempt to found a real old-time community; just possibly he was satisfied to remember the one he had actually known. A handful of others remained, Harry watching the boat each day from the post office and Guy and Ray heading into the hills with their strings of horses. There were newcomers as before. Some made downlake demands and left in disillusion. But there were others who caught the notes of awe and laughter that were the valley's own. And for all who would see or hear, there remained those older presences, McGregor and the river, with all they had to tell.

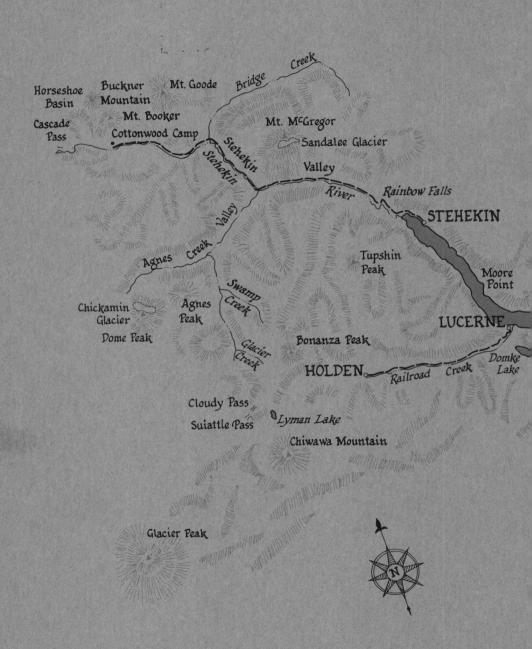

Horseshoe
Basin

Buckner
Mountain

Mt. Goode

Bridge   Creek

Cascade
Pass

Mt. Booker

Cottonwood Camp

Mt. McGregor

Sandalee Glacier

Stehekin

Valley

Stehekin

Valley

Stehekin   River   Rainbow Falls

STEHEKIN

Tupshin
Peak

Moore
Point

Agnes   Creek

Chickamin
Glacier

Agnes
Peak

Swamp
Creek

Dome Peak

Glacier
Creek

Bonanza Peak

LUCERNE

HOLDEN   Railroad   Creek

Domke
Lake

Cloudy Pass

Suiattle Pass

Lyman Lake

Chiwawa Mountain

Glacier Peak

N

0 1 2 3 4 5 miles